Geoffrey Wooler

To Don.

Happy 40th 1959 - 1999

Gosh how time flies

Love Maggie

xx

PIG IN A SUITCASE

Pig in a Suitcase

Geoffrey Wooler

First published in 1999 by
Smith Settle Ltd
Ilkley Road
Otley
West Yorkshire
LS21 3JP

ISBN 1 85825 111 7

British Library Cataloguing-in-Publication data:
A catalogue record for this book is available from the British Library.

Designed, printed and bound by
SMITH SETTLE
Ilkley Road, Otley, West Yorkshire LS21 3JP

Contents

Acknowledgements

No words that I know can express the thanks I owe to Janet and Malcolm Barker. Their friendly advice and daily encouragement were responsible for my continuing to do something I have never attempted before. I am deeply grateful for the tremendous help they have given me.

I cannot type, nor can I dictate spontaneously with a tape recorder, so I wrote the whole text in longhand which took over two years. Fortunately Mrs Ann Dixon, secretary to my nephew Peter Wooler, after considerable practice was able to read my writing, and with the aid of a computer produced a result which everybody can understand. I am grateful for her coming to my rescue.

Professor Harry Shumacker has written a flattering introduction and it is difficult to believe that it could really be me.

My thanks go to Miss Stanka Kraljevic for sending me details of the history of Korcula, particularly in the 16th and 17th centuries. Neven Fazinic kindly photographed places of interest in Korcula for me which have a British connection.

The portrait of Professor William Wright, and the photos of Queen Mary's visit to the London Hospital, are reproduced by permission of the Custodian of the Royal London Hospital Archives. The photograph of the Urn in Westminster Abbey containing the bones of the two Princes was sent to me by the Keeper of the Muniments in Westminster Abbey. The cartoon 'There's no business like show business' is by Garland of the *Daily Telegraph*. Some photographs were taken for the *Yorkshire Post* and *Evening Post*; for these, many thanks.

My nephew the Rev. Michael Hepper has continued to give me helpful advice. It is he who gave the book its title.

Mr Christopher Slater, master at Leeds Grammar School, translated the Latin verse on the stone tablet at the entrance to my house in Korcula.

Princess Orietta Doria Pamphilj kindly sent me the text of her father's speech which he gave after the liberation of Rome in 1994.

Lastly the publisher, Mr Ken Smith, has been so patient with me that he well deserves a word of thanks from an amateur.

Introduction

In recording incidents in his long and interesting life, Mr Geoffrey Wooler has given us a real treat.

Few have had such varied and fascinating experiences, and fewer still could record them with such good humour.

This well-travelled Yorkshire surgeon has said comparatively little about his role in introducing 'Surgery of the Heart' to England: and instead has related fascinating and amusing events in which he has played a part or been an interested bystander.

Pig in a Suitcase does not simply hold the reader's undivided attention — it demands more — and from the tales he tells, and from what his friends know to be true, the author could have continued indefinitely. Certainly as the reader closes the book he is left with an appetite for more.

Harris B. Shumacker
M.D., D.Sc. (hon.), F.A.C.S, Hon. F.R.C.S. (Eng),
Lieut-Colonel U.S. Army (retired)
Distinguished Professor of Surgery in the
Uniformed Services University and in Indiana University

Dedication

To my very dear mother and father,
Ethel Pauline and George Hartley Wooler.

I

Childhood and Student Days

My family has lived in Leeds for over two hundred years. We have a Marriage Certificate dated 22nd December, 1778, between Hannah Wainwright and John Wooler at Leeds Parish Church. Then follows a fairly complete collection of Certificates of Baptism and Marriage until the present time, most of the ceremonies taking place in the Leeds Parish Church, also Death Certificates: but like all families the Woolers have had their ups and downs.

I was born on 24th November, 1911. My father, George Hartley Wooler, was a successful businessman who managed to stabilise the finances for his wife and children. My mother, Ethel Pauline, whose father was a quarry owner, was unfortunately blind. She contracted an infection when my brother, Edwin John Loy Wooler, was born which affected her eyes and she lost her sight. It was seven years after the birth of my brother that my parents decided to have an addition to the family and I was the next to arrive. My sister Joyce was born a few years later and she was the youngest. Because of my mother's disability I was looked after by a nursemaid called Winnie. She taught me to knit and crochet which indeed eighty years later I can still perform. I like to think that my surgical technique later in life was fostered at an early age by Winnie teaching me the intricacies of crocheting and knitting.

I attended a private kindergarten school run by four sisters, the Misses Newman. They were all spinsters and they had a fifth sister who was happily married and had three children. Their father was a retired Methodist Minister who always wore a black suit and was never seen without a Bible or some religious book in his hand. From the age of nine until I was thirteen years old I attended Leeds Grammar School, where regrettably I made a bad impression when I joined the Wolf Cubs. In 1921 each Wolf Cub wore a simple uniform and carried a long pole which was his prize possession, enabling him to leap over streams etc. Returning home after my third Cub meeting I left my pole on the tramcar. About two weeks later my parents were informed that the pole had been found and was at the tram depot. Having attended two Cub meetings without my precious pole, before the next meeting took place my father escorted

Geoffrey Wooler and his sister Joyce at Shadwell, their parents' home, in 1919.

me to the tram depot himself, collected the pole, and left me at the school safely with it. The Cub leader, who had previously reprimanded me, looked pleased when he saw I was properly equipped; but returning home on the tram from the meeting, I was stupid enough to leave it again. My father refused to co-operate any more so when I appeared at school again without a pole I was accused of being careless, of not showing interest in the Wolf Cub movement, and I was given my discharge.

My parents were musical, my father was an excellent violinist and my mother, in spite of her disability, played the piano extremely well. They hoped I would follow their example so when I attended the kindergarten school, one of the Misses Newman taught me to play the piano. At first I looked promising and during my first year at the Leeds Grammar School I played Beethoven's 1st Piano Sonata at a school concert and was awarded a prize, but the talent I had apparently inherited from my parents came to a halt and regrettably I made no further progress. However, my having won a music prize at the early age of nine alerted members of my family, so that when one of them died I was always bequeathed their piano, possibly because at this time they were of little value and difficult to sell. At one stage I was housing five, four uprights and one boudoir grand, all of German manufacture and fine instruments. I

A family group at Shadwell: (back row left to right) Geoffrey Wooler, Joyce Wooler and E. J. Loy Wooler; (front) mother, Mrs Ethel Wooler, and father, Mr George Wooler.

gradually disposed of them and I am sure they were pleased to have new homes because with me they performed nothing more exciting than Beethoven's 1st Piano Sonata.

We were a happy family; my mother's disability appeared to rivet us together as a team, everybody helping with the chores in the house and garden. Sunday morning we attended Church properly dressed for the occasion, and when I was a child Winnie would accompany us to look after me, which was not easy because I used to crawl forward under the pews and make for the choir. Sunday mid-day dinner always consisted of roast beef and Yorkshire pudding, usually followed by apple pie. There was a pause before we commenced eating while my father said the Grace. The meat course was finished in relative silence because we were hungry but the arrival of the apple pie was a signal for my brother and my father to crack jokes at one another. Both of them had a marvellous sense of humour and we could not eat for laughing. Mother fortunately came to the rescue, interrupting them because the pie was getting cold. I never heard my parents blaspheme or swear and only on one occasion when something had really irritated my father badly did I hear him say 'Oh sugar it'. Every day of his life he looked after my mother and he was never separated from her. Even when she was admitted to the Harley Street Clinic under Sir James Walton, my father was also admitted, taking the room adjoining hers so that he could be with her before and after the operation for a suspected cancer. Incidentally, while my mother and father were in this Clinic, Barbara Hutton, the Woolworth heiress, was admitted to a room opposite theirs. She was escaping from her second husband who was maltreating her. She had left him in the house she had built in Regent's Park, what a complete contrast with the way my parents behaved.

I went to Giggleswick School when I was thirteen years old to find that I was the youngest boarder at the school, and my first year was rather strange and a bit tough. I had never been away from home before and there were a number of Victorian customs still in progress — fagging was one of them, which was supposed to teach you obedience and cleanliness. A new boy was assigned to a prefect for cleaning his shoes, tidying his study and performing other duties demanded by him. If a fag was considered to be inefficient or disobeyed orders he was given punishment drill. However, at the end of the term the boys had a chance of getting their own back on the prefects who had treated them badly. The whole school would line up at each side of the corridor armed with gym shoes and other suitable weapons. The prefects would walk or run between the two lines along the whole length of this corridor and the unpopular ones would arrive at the end in a bruised condition. This was embarrassing for anyone

Geoffrey Wooler's parents, George and Ethel Wooler, in the rose garden at Shadwell.

who showed signs of disfigurement because immediately after this episode the prefects dined with all the masters at an end of term farewell party.

At Giggleswick I was unfortunate in following my brother Loy. He was an exceptionally good rugger player and captained the first team for two years when they had one success after another. When I arrived at Giggleswick, for having the name Wooler I was immediately assigned to the Colts first team, but it was not for long. I was really hopeless at the game and disliked it. After rude remarks from the touchline it was obvious to everybody that I was not another Loy, so after my third game with the Colts, and greatly to my relief, I was dropped and did not need to try and play any more Rugby football.

After the first year, I enjoyed my other five at the school very much. I became friendly with a boy who lived in the Cheviot Hills in Northumberland. We used to go long walks together in the surrounding countryside and he taught me a lot about wildlife and wild flowers. The interests which he created have remained with me all my life, they were certainly more peaceful and more pleasant than fighting on a Rugby field.

The headmaster at Giggleswick was a Mr. R.N. Douglas. He had a quite outstanding student career at Cambridge University, obtaining a double first in Classics, and becoming a triple blue by representing the University at Rugby football, cricket and tennis. I have never heard of anyone else achieving so much. He was a devout Christian and every morning after breakfast he led the whole school in prayer. Evening prayers were taken by the housemaster before retiring to bed. Sunday was a day of rest except for morning and evening services in the Chapel where everybody attended properly dressed in black suits and stiff white collars.

Mr. Douglas was ordained after he retired from the school and went to a small parish somewhere in South Devon. The teaching at Giggleswick was excellent and responsible for me attaining eleven credits in the School Certificate examination. Mr. Douglas spoke to my father and strongly advised him to allow me to go to his old college in Cambridge which was Selwyn. The results of the School Certificate exempted me from taking the Cambridge entrance examination except for the subject of Latin, which I hated. Most surprisingly however, at the first opportunity I did pass in Latin, and then was accepted as a student at Selwyn College. I was in a dilemma because I had not decided what subjects to study at the University and they were expecting me in six months' time. My father quite rightly refused to influence me in making this decision, saying that anything leading on to my future career must be decided by myself. At about this time my brother Loy passed his final examinations to become a lawyer, and I thought that as he was successful, I had a chance of doing the same and perhaps later on joining him in a partnership. So, without knowing or asking details about the Law Course at Cambridge, I wrote to Selwyn College asking to become a law student and was accepted.

In October, 1930, when I arrived in Cambridge, to my dismay I found that for the first two years I should be studying Roman law in its original Latin and practically nothing else. I still have the institutes of Gaius and Justinian here in my house and nobody in the family seems to be interested in them, even though we have had two lawyers, so the books have not been opened for about sixty years.

The excitement of being a fresher at Cambridge masked my resentment of studying two years of Latin and I went ahead with the course of the LL.B. John McKeller, who was one of my friends at Giggleswick School, had accompanied me to Cambridge, and he also resided at Selwyn College. He was reading medicine, hoping later to join his father in general practice in Dewsbury. My course in law dragged on and I was not enjoying it. One evening my tutor in Roman law told us that he was most distressed with an interview he had had that day with a father of one of the law students. The tutor had been told in an unpleasant way that he was wasting our time and his money by teaching us Roman law. The tutor then removed his spectacles and looked at us saying 'Gentlemen, I want you to be cultured lawyers, not just lawyers'. I was beginning to think that I had had enough of culture and towards the end of my second term I enquiried whether I would be allowed to change to another subject. One wet afternoon, through lack of anything better to do, John McKeller took me on a tour of the departments of anatomy and physiology in the medical school. These places fascinated me and I was determined to change to medicine as soon as possible. My tutor at Selwyn College gave his consent on condition that my parents first agreed, which indeed they did, my father saying that he didn't care what I did as long as I was of use to the community and didn't waste my time.

Returning to Cambridge after the Easter vacation, I was allowed to remain a student as long as I passed all four parts of the first examination for Bachelor of Medicine quickly. These subjects are normally taken at school but I had no trouble with them and then commenced to study anatomy and physiology for the second part, which I passed at the end of my third year, obtaining at the same time an ordinary BA degree.

Lord Moran, the Dean of St. Mary's Hospital, London, invited all third year students of both Oxford and Cambridge Universities to dinner in order to persuade them to select St. Mary's for their clinical work. He was particularly interested in anybody who could play Rugby football, and to those who were good at the game he would offer a scholarship. This was the first time I had heard of a player being paid for his ability to play football. As a result, St. Mary's had a first class team and invariably won the inter-hospital Rugby football competition. Only the Dean, cheering from the touchline wearing a beaver coat and pork pie hat, knew how much they had cost.

In October, 1933, I went to the London Hospital in Whitechapel to do my clinical work. It was the largest voluntary hospital in Britain, having over one thousand beds. The combined out-patient clinics had an average attendance of three hundred patients daily, so there was ample scope for learning all branches of medicine and surgery.

The hospital was built in the latter half of the eighteenth century. Originally it had only one operating theatre where the table was covered with a large sheet of leather which was washed down after each operation. Before my student days in the 1930s a block of six operating theatres had been built on the top of the original building, a position which provided plenty of natural light at a time when electric operating lamps were not very efficient. Each surgeon had his own operating theatre and as their individual tastes varied considerably, each theatre had its own character and interest. Mr. Russell Howard, being the senior surgeon, had Theatre No.1. It showed evidence of the Listerian period because on the shelves high up on the surrounding walls were large glass cisterns with the inscriptions on them '1 in 20 Acid Carbol, 1 in 100 Acid Carbol', the same concentrations Lord Lister had advocated in his article which appeared in *The Lancet* in 1865 commencing the technique of antiseptic surgery. I never saw the cisterns used and probably as well for they must have been in the theatre for about forty years, Russell Howard having in all probability inherited them from his predecessor. His theatre demonstrated that he didn't easily accept new ideas. When he arrived to operate he removed only his jacket, donned a rubber apron to protect his trousers, his waistcoat and gold Albert, and never changed his shoes. After scrubbing up he put on a sterile gown, a cap, and a mask which he always wore below his nose because he complained that he couldn't otherwise breathe. He was never anxious to wear rubber gloves, saying that they interfered with his touch, and I think he was probably right. In those days the rubber gloves were similar to the thick kitchen gloves worn today for washing up pots and pans. We had no air conditioning in the theatre, and even on the hottest days, with all his clothes covered with a rubber apron, I never saw him sweat. The large glass windows in the ceiling could be a nuisance during the summer. Russell Howard was an excellent teacher and I learned a great deal from him. His motto was 'Surgery is only anatomy and common sense'.

Sir Henry Souttar had the operating theatre next to Mr. Russell Howard. Inside he housed a large mahogany Georgian glass-fronted bookcase which contained the instruments he had made himself. The attic of his house in Harley Street was an engineering workshop where he produced many ingenious and some extremely useful instruments. He earned the title of the Flying Surgeon, because in the 1930s he flew to India with Dr. Challis, his anaesthetist, in order to remove the cancerous growth from an Indian princess's tongue. The operation was performed in the library of the palace, and leading down into the library from the floor above there was a spiral iron staircase. Just as Dr. Challis commenced the anaesthetic he was disturbed by a loud clanging noise caused by the prince's sword catching on each step as he descended into the library.

Sir James Walton, surgeon to the Royal household, had the next theatre which was always kept beautifully clean and tidy. He was a very fast and an extremely good surgeon. He would not allow blood transfusions to be given to his patients because he considered it was an insult to his technique if any blood was lost. One day two Americans arrived with a sort of small mobile sewing machine which they wanted him to buy, saying it would lessen the time of doing an intestinal anastamosis by fifteen minutes. Sir James performed the operation in fourteen minutes on the the next patient. The Americans watching the procedure remarked afterwards, 'I guess you don't require our machine after all' and they took it to another hospital.

Sir James' hobby was cutting diamonds. He was certainly proficient because the merchants of Hatton Gardens frequently sent him their wares, presumably when they thought that the work was too difficult for them.

He was also an accomplished gymnast. In order to celebrate a long successful operation he would do a handspring over the operating table to demonstrate that he still had plenty of energy left.

An interesting person was the cranial surgeon, Sir Hugh Cairns. One of his operations might last the whole day and during this time his poor lady anaesthetist would be completely covered over with the operating sheets, making it impossible for her to avoid inhaling the anaesthetic. She always looked dazed when she finally emerged from the covers.

Before going to Oxford as Nuffield Professor of Surgery, Sir Hugh attended Lawrence of Arabia after he had crashed with his motor bicycle but unfortunately he died.

The gynaecological and midwifery course for students lasted three months. In the lecture theatre one day we were awaiting the arrival of Mr. Eardley Holland, the Senior Gynaecologist, who was about ten minutes late. He appeared immaculately dressed in a morning suit and before beginning his talk, he produced a sponge bag from the tail pocket of his jacket. A very ordinary lump of meat fell on to the table from the sponge bag, as he remarked: 'Gentlemen, I thought you might be interested to see a duchess's uterus.' It is the only time I have seen the tail pocket of a morning suit used as a sort of game bag.

Mr. Holland was always in favour of not interfering with nature but allowing it to take its own course. He told the students one day about when he was called out to see a Countess who was approaching full term for delivery of her child. She insisted on being delivered by Caesarian section because she did not wish to go into labour. Both her local general practitioner and a local gynaecologist saw no reason why the child should not be delivered normally, so Mr. Holland from London was called in for a third opinion and, after examining the lady, he too saw no reason for advising birth by Caesarian section. The Countess was very persistent and was not satisfied with his answer and she requested to see someone else. There was in Paris a Professor of Gynaecology who had an international reputation so Mr. Holland asked him to come and see the patient. The Parisian Professor examined her and confirmed what the previous Consultants had advised but being French he was able to explain the situation in a more flamboyant fashion, saying to her 'My lady, if you were in a room and you wished to go out, would you climb through the window or walk out of the door?' The Countess naturally replied that she would certainly go through the door and he said 'Well that is the way your baby is going to arrive'.

During the last month of the course we were assigned to a fully qualified and experienced midwife who took all the responsibility for our actions but, in order to impress the patients, addressed us as doctor and we had to do the work. Pregnant women, attending the outpatients of the London Hospital regularly, were graded according to whether their pregnancies were considered to be straightforward or likely to present a slight problem when labour commenced. The absolutely straightforward cases were told that they would be delivered in their own homes, by a midwife and a doctor (so-called). This part of our training was called 'working on the district'. From the London Hospital this meant attending cases in such areas as Wapping, Limehouse, and Bethnal Green, all interesting places even before the war. It was also good for our morale because it taught responsibility which we certainly needed later on when qualified.

I remember two incidents when I was working on the district. The first one occurred in a small house in Limehouse, a sort of one up and one down abode. I took the midwife there in my car and she brought the necessary equipment with her which contained only one pair of sterile gloves and one gown. After being introduced as the doctor I scrubbed up, donned the only sterile gown and my one pair of rubber gloves, then sat on a stool waiting for things to happen. Everything seemed to be so slow, and it was only after about one hour we became optimistic. However, during this period I began to feel uncomfortable; having sat on a low stool for almost an hour, my trousers had gradually been drawn up with the long wait so I stood up to let them fall down into a more comfortable position. The midwife, thinking that I was about to deliver the baby standing up, took my stool away without warning, and I sat down with a loud bang on the floor, unable to protect the fall because I did not wish to dirty my one pair of sterile gloves. The house shook, and the husband rushed upstairs thinking his wife had fallen out of bed but we reassured him, and all went well, including the delivery.

The other incident happened in a small terraced house at Wapping, not very far from the Prospect of Whitby public house. I was called to see a lady who had already had four children without any difficulty and I was to deliver the fifth, but it didn't go according to plan. She had been in labour for a very long time, the midwife thought it wise to telephone the hospital and send for the surgical first assistant, who had the status of a Junior Consultant. He was a well built man from Australia, who was used to a wild life in the bush. He was captain of the hospital rugger team, and because of the size of his shoulders, he was the hooker in the football scrum. We explained everything to him and he decided that forceps were necessary to help the delivery. I stepped aside while he applied the forceps, a moderate pull produced no result, so with his feet firmly on the floor, he put all his strength into the next pull. The forceps slipped off the child's head, and he went through a plaster wall into the next house. Except for the hole in the wall, all turned out well, the baby being delivered by hand eventually. It is the only time I have seen the dividing wall of a house made of wooden laths and plaster like the construction of a ceiling.

There was a General Election in 1936. One of the Senior Consultants at the London Hospital decided to stand as a Conservative Candidate for an East End constituency. He was Dr. O'Donovan, head of the Department of Dermatology, who had one of the largest out-patient clinics at the hospital. Not infrequently patients with venereal disease would present with a rash and be seen at his clinic, then transferred to the appropriate department.

The East End of London was a hotbed of Communism and considered an absolutely safe seat for anyone with such beliefs. Dr. O'Donovan was a brave man to confront them, but he was quick witted and an excellent orator, so that when he toured the East End in an open car he had an answer to everyone who challenged his views. As he was well known as a doctor, and respected, nothing unpleasant was thrown at him. The final meeting was held at the Queen's Theatre in Poplar. About ten of us from the London Hospital decided to attend and give him our support. The theatre was absolutely full, but there seemed to be few supporters of the Conservative Party present apart from ourselves. O'Donovan was undaunted and answered every remark that was made. When it became obvious that he was winning the audience on to his side, a tough looking young man with a thick red face and an open-necked red shirt stood up in the middle of the audience, pointed to O'Donovan and shouted, 'Look at him, the pox doctor'. O'Donovan immediately replied: 'I thought I had seen your face before'. He was elected and I think was the first and the last Conservative candidate to become a Member of Parliament for the East End of London.

Professor William Wright was Dean of the Medical School at the London Hospital and he was also Professor of Anatomy at the London University. He became famous after he had dissected and published the anatomy of the elephant's trunk, finding that it contained no fewer than four hundred different muscles. When he had finished with the different portions of the trunk, he asked the attendant in the dissecting room of the Department of Anatomy to dispose of the bits. The attendant decided that the easiest way was to add portions of the elephant to the dissected human remains in each coffin before burial. Unfortunately, too much of the elephant had been added to one of the coffins for safety. The lid was not screwed down properly and sprang open just before it was buried. The contents were obviously not human and eventually the Bishop of London was informed of what had happened. Burying an elephant in holy ground might have been unthinkable, but was impossible to rectify without exhuming all the other coffins which had come from the same source. Finally, nothing was done and the embarrassing incident was kept secret, and the assistant in the anatomical department was reprimanded but did not lose his job. Professor Wright became President of the Anatomical Society, and the elephant's trunk remained in holy ground.

Professor William Wright, Dean of the Medical School at London Hospital, in 1938.

The Dean and authorities of Westminster Abbey commissioned Professor Wright to open the urn which supposedly contained the bones of the two Princes murdered in the Tower by their uncle, King Richard III, in 1483. The urn had never been opened before. As well as human remains, it was found to contain a considerable number of chicken and animal bones, the explanation being that after the murder, the two boys were buried hurriedly in the ground near to the kitchen of the Tower. Then, later on, when it was decided that they should be buried in the Abbey, their remains were exhumed and whoever did this was unable to differentiate between human and other bones from the kitchen. The animal and chicken bones were discarded by Professor Wright and the human ones examined carefully. They proved extremely interesting. They were of two boys who were almost certainly brothers because both their skulls presented a very rare anomaly, which was an extra bone in the cranium, called a Wormium bone. This finding proved beyond doubt that they were of the same family. Examination of the development of the long bones showed that they had died when they were thirteen and eleven years old which would be in 1483, when history states that the Princes were murdered. After obtaining as much information as possible, the bones were cleaned, lacquered to preserve them, and then wrapped in two layers of pure white linen before being replaced into the urn, which was then sealed. Soon after Professor Wright had carried out this work he became ill himself, complaining of severe back ache and an x-ray showed that he had multiple carcinomatosis deposits in his spine. I think he died without publishing these findings of the two Princes, but the lecture he gave at the London Hospital Medical School is one I shall always vividly remember.

The urn in Westminster Abbey containing the bones of the two princes. (©Dean & Chapter of Westminster)

I qualified with the London Conjoint Examination in 1937 and passed the Cambridge MB BCh the following year.

My first resident appointment at the London Hospital was house surgeon to the Ear, Nose & Throat Department which had four Consulting Surgeons, the senior one being Mr. Norman Patterson. He was outstanding technically, and well ahead of his time with his surgical skill and procedures; but he had one drawback, and that was being very forgetful. Having long lists of tonsillectomies and nasal operations, I had to make sure that the correct operation was performed on each patient, otherwise one might wake up without his tonsils when part of his nasal septum should have been removed. This did happen once when I was his house surgeon. Surprisingly the patient did not appear to mind losing his tonsils, and seemed grateful: which certainly would not happen to-day. On more than one occasion Mr. Patterson would forget about his car and chauffeur waiting in the hospital car park, and return to his home in Harley Street by the underground, his chauffeur then coming to ask me what had happened to his chief. He was not a tall gentleman. One day, as I was escorting him from the Consultants' cloakroom to the front door of the hospital, I couldn't help noticing that the overcoat he had just put on was much too big for him and was trailing on the floor. After I mentioned it he returned to the cloakroom, and re-appeared with his own coat.

One morning after we had seen all the out-patients and were having tea quietly in the Sisters' room, Mr. Patterson suddenly got up and left, saying that he had an important appointment and was already late. He returned a few moments later because he had forgotten his hat. We settled down again, Mr. Morris, who was the second surgeon, reading spicy bits out of the *Daily Mirror* and I talking to Sister, when the door flew open again, Mr. Patterson re-appearing saying he had left some important papers. Mr. Morris looked over the top of the *Daily Mirror* and said 'Look in your hat', and sure enough there they were.

The London Hospital had a dining room used by the Consultants, the junior doctors and the administrative staff. This excellent idea allowed the three different categories to meet and get to know one another. The Chairman of the London Hospital was Sir John Mann, who owned a brewery in the East End, and supplied free beer to everyone using the dining room. This generosity was never abused, and I rarely saw more than half the diners ask for it.

The administrative staff at the London were all ex-servicemen holding on to their official titles. One day I was lunching with Maurice Young, House Physician to Sir Arthur Ellis, who was Professor of Medicine at the hospital. We had just started to eat when Sir Arthur came into the dining room looking for his House Physician but when he saw the administrative staff there he went to speak to them first, saying 'Good morning Commander Laird, good morning Captain Brierley, good morning Colonel Cahusac' and finally, turning to his House Physician said 'Hello you little b-----, how are you'.

Sir Arthur was interested in a metabolic disorder called tetany caused by lowering the blood calcium. If Dr. Young admitted such a case he was to inform Sir Arthur immediately before commencing treatment. One evening a suitable case was admitted, and when he telephoned his chief in Harley Street, Dr. Young was told by the housekeeper that Sir Arthur was dining out, but she would inform him immediately. About twenty minutes later he arrived at the hospital in full Court dress, for he was attending the Lord Mayor's Banquet at the Guildhall. After he had examined the patient and detailed the course of treatment, Dr. Young escorted him to the front door of the hospital where there was a large Rolls Royce limousine waiting. Dr. Young opened the back door of the car whereupon Sir Arthur turned to him and said 'Thank you very much, Young, but it's much safer for me to drive from the front'.

The Senior Anaesthetist at the London Hospital was a Dr. Astley Cooper, locally known as Daddy Cooper. He initiated me into the art of giving a general anaesthetic by the old-fashioned method of dropping ether or chloroform on to a gauze face mask, the so-called rag and bottle method. Dr. Cooper, seeing that I was rather nervous giving my first anaesthetic, came and sat beside me saying 'Now just a few drops, take it slowly' but this was quickly followed by a loud command 'Go on, go on', at the same time nudging me to be more active. Then, dissatisfied with my slowness, he took over from me and continued to pour ether on to the face mask until every muscle of the patient was absolutely flaccid, making it easy for the surgeon to do almost anything he wished. As it was my first anaesthetic experience I thought that the patient looked almost dead and I was pleasantly surprised when I saw him come round from the anaesthetic and look reasonably well. This method was known amongst the students as 'Cooperisation'.

Another eminent physician on the staff of the London Hospital was Lord Evans, previously known as Dr. Horace Evans. He became Consulting Physician to Her Majesty Queen Mary, and once told me how he had attained such an eminent position. When Queen Mary was short of a medical advisor, it appears she used to invite all prospective candidates to lunch with her one at a time in Buckingham Palace. Prior to this interview Lord Evans, realising Queen Mary was mad about antiques, of which he had little knowledge himself, spent all the available time studying books on antique furniture and visiting the antique shops in Bond Street, etc. At lunch Queen Mary was delighted to find that she discovered a doctor who actually had the same interests as herself and immediately appointed him. Evans had a marvellous sense of humour. One day I was accompanying him on a ward round at the London Hospital, where he had been requested to see a middle-aged man with shortness of breath. After going through the numerous investigations which had been performed, his House Physician noticed that Evans was examining an electrocardiographic tracing of the heart, holding it upside down. The young resident doctor, unwilling to embarrass his chief, waited for the opportune moment when he thought nobody was looking, then gradually turned the electrocardiograph the right way up. Lord Evans felt the adjustment and turning to the House Physician said 'You know, in order to be proficient, you need to interpret these recordings in any position.'

The East End of London before the War provided few leisure facilities. There were swimming baths at Aldgate, but they were small and always crowded and the baths at Holborn were the nearest acceptable ones. About a mile from the hospital was the East End Park. It amazed me that anything green could survive in soil which had been contaminated for over a hundred years with soot. It always looked dismal and uninviting. Grass and laurel bushes appeared to be the only plants to survive. They were suitable for a graveyard rather than a pleasure park, but there were several interesting pubs in the East End all worth visiting. The bar at Dirty Dick's near Liverpool Street was full of different types of cobwebs for anyone interested in spiders. Charlie Chan's in Limehouse had a stuffed bear to greet new arrivals. Most interesting of all was the Prospect of Whitby in Wapping on the North bank of the Thames, which had a veranda built out on to the river bank from which to watch the shipping and the activity of the docks. The students and resident doctors always held their farewell dinner parties at the Prospect in a large room on the first floor facing the river. When I first knew the place nothing inside the pub had ever been changed and the atmosphere was excellent. I remember taking a friend of mine, Bernard Cayzer, there one night for a meal. He was a director of the Union Castle Shipping Line, the Cayzer Irving Shipping Company, and other concerns too numerous to mention. We had an excellent meal and after dinner four young sailors started to sing sea shanties and danced a clog dance which I had never seen done before in England.

Princess Margaret took a party of friends for dinner one evening to the Prospect which caused the whole atmosphere of the place to change. The owners refurbished it with cheap reproduction furniture and new lighting, ruining its character. Previously it was Dickensian, now it was ridiculous.

I was sad when my appointment with the Ear, Nose & Throat Department finished. I applied and was accepted as resident to Mr. Tudor Edwards. He had just been invited to join the Consultants' Staff at the London Hospital in order to commence a Thoracic Surgical Unit. Thoracic surgery in 1938 was a new speciality which the physicians resented. Heart and lung diseases were their preserves and to attack them surgically was an insult to their ability and pride. It was particularly resented by the Medical Superintendents of the Tuberculosis Sanatoria. To cure their patients would be to deprive them of their jobs and livelihoods, so this new species of surgeons must be kept at bay for as long as possible. Fortunately, Mr. Tudor Edwards did not encounter too many of these rebuffs. He was always tactful in his remarks, and was accepted as an exceptionally fine and gifted surgeon.

It was however most unfortunate that, at about the middle of my resident

Tudor Edwards (second from right) and his wife Eve (right) entertaining Sir Geoffrey and Lady Todd at their country house near Petworth in 1938.

appointment, Mr. Tudor Edwards had his first heart attack just after returning by car from Grenoble where he had been presented with an honorary MD degree at the University. We didn't see him for nearly two months. On his return, while I was attending his out-patient clinic, one of his patients, who had previously been operated on by him, turned pale and looking at Tudor remarked 'Coo'er I didn't expect to see you again'. Tudor replied 'Well, I am here'. He inherited one interesting patient who had previously been treated by a general surgeon. The patient had started with an abscess in his chest which had been drained by inserting a tube through the chest wall. The drainage proved inadequate, resulting in the infection eroding lung tissue and rupturing into a bronchus. The patient had now a communication between a bronchus and the original drainage tube in his chest wall, enabling him to breathe through it. He usually kept a cork in this hole because breathing through his mouth and nose was more efficient. The chest hole was useful particularly in the East End pubs. He would bet new clients unknown to him that he could hold his head under water much longer than they could. Having knocked the cork out of the chest hole with his elbow, he always won.

Tudor and his wife, Eve, loved entertaining. After a heavy and successful day he would invite you out to dinner, usually at the Mayfair Restaurant, where the head chef was Signor Cassaldi, who had been his patient. During the first World War, Cassaldi was in the Italian Army and received a chest wound at the Battle of Caporetto. The wound had never healed and continued to discharge pus, until 20 years later, Tudor explored it, removed part of Cassaldi's tunic, and it healed.

I was sad when my appointment with Tudor Edwards finished. He had given me encouragement and made me think that perhaps, after all, I too might be able to operate successfully.

My third residency followed with Mr. Russell Howard, the Senior Consulting Surgeon, and a wonderful teacher. Even though his methods were a bit antiquated, they were still important. While working for him we admitted another rather unusual case which on the admission sheet stated that it was for excision of haemorrhoids. At operation the patient was found to have a prolongation of his skin from the tip of his coccyx, giving an appearance of a six inch long tail. The surgeon excised this at the same time as dealing with his piles but the patient was furious when he was told. Like the man with the hole in his chest he had been going round the East End pubs winning drinks with his tail, now he would never forgive the surgeon for docking him, and depriving him of free beer.

I joined the Territorial Army in September 1938, being appointed Medical Officer to the 2nd Battalion the Queen's Westminsters. Unfortunately for me, when the war started I had not completed my surgical training at the London Hospital. When the Mobilisation Order arrived I was working as resident to Mr. Russell Howard at the London Hospital. He strongly advised me to stay with him in order to finish my training and pass the final examination of the Fellowship before becoming a soldier. Mr. Howard was in a powerful position, with considerable authority, as he had been appointed surgeon in charge of Section 1 of the Emergency Medical Service. Perhaps foolishly, I declined his offer, informing him that I knew almost every member of the 2nd Battalion of the Queen's Westminsters and didn't wish to desert them at this time. In any case, I told him I thought the war would last no longer than one or two years and I would return to work for him when it was over.

2

Arrested in Berlin

During the autumn of 1938 I had a free period of about six weeks between two house surgical appointments. One of my chiefs, Mr. Tudor Edwards, suggested I should go and visit Professor Sauerbuch's Clinic at the Charité Hospital in Berlin to which I readily agreed because I knew one of his assistants, Dr. Hans Brink. He had been a medical student with me at Cambridge University and we were great friends. Sauerbuch was at the height of his career as Professor of Surgery at Berlin University. He was also a friend and surgeon to Adolf Hitler.

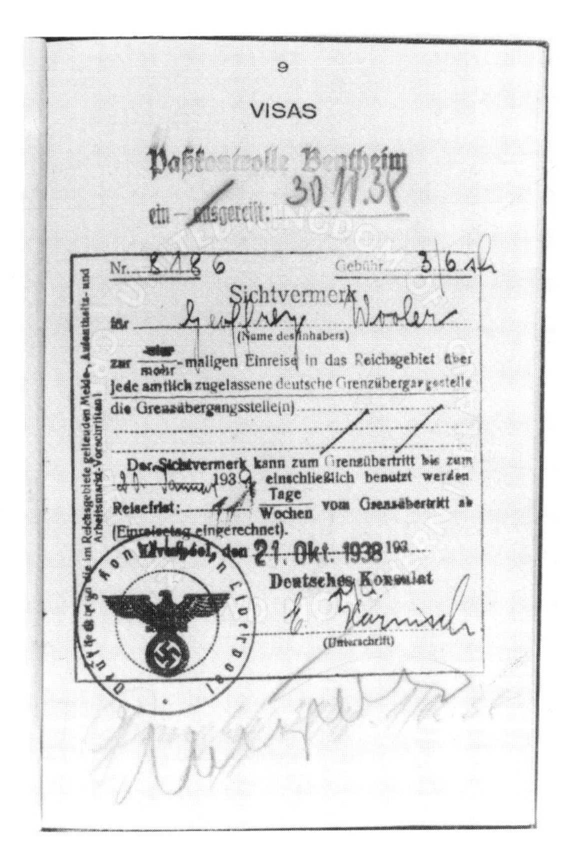
9

VISAS

Paßkontrolle Bentheim

ein— ausgereist: 30.11.38

Nr. 8186 Gebühr 3/6

Sichtvermerk

für Geoffrey Wooler

(Name des Inhabers)

zur mehr-maligen Einreise in das Reichsgebiet über jede amtlich zugelassene deutsche Grenzübergangsstelle

die Grenzübergangsstelle(n)

Der Sichtvermerk kann zum Grenzübertritt bis zum 1939 einschließlich benutzt werden.

Reisefrist: Tage / Wochen vom Grenzübertritt ab (Einreisetag eingerechnet).

den 21. Okt. 1938

Deutsches Konsulat

(Unterschrift)

The visa granted to Geoffrey Wooler to enter Germany in 1938.

I decided to go from Harwich to the Hook of Holland and then through Holland by train into Germany. I went to Cannon Street Station with my suitcase, bought my ticket and was shown my train which was waiting at one of the platforms. I was told that it would not leave for at least one and a half hours; so I left my suitcase in a corner seat of one of the carriages and went to the station café to have some coffee. While I was drinking my coffee I was horrified to see the train leaving the station with my luggage in it. The station master telephoned Harwich for me and when I arrived there about an hour later my suitcase was safely waiting for me. After crossing the

Channel I boarded a train at the Hook of Holland which would take me to Germany. I travelled second class. I shared a compartment with some Canadian girls whom I had seen perform at the Palace Theatre in London giving a sort of cabaret show on ice. They were called Juanita and her Girls. There were five or six of them including one exceedingly small girl who during the performance was swung around in a circle in mid air while a much stronger one held securely on to her feet. At the frontier crossing into Germany they were reprimanded by a German soldier for throwing empty ice cream cartons on to the platform, and I must say I agreed with the soldier.

I left the train to spend two days in Hanover for I wanted to see the Veterinary College which supposedly was the best in Europe, and it certainly impressed me. The girls continued on to Berlin where they were to perform at the Wintergarten. A friend of Hans Brink looked after me in Hanover and accommodated me in the medical students' hostel. The occupants were anxious to impress a stranger from England but their constant request was for the British to restore Tanganyika to German rule. One of the young doctors had been born there. He was enormously tall and his nickname was 'Emu', but he was an aggressive character and I am sure was a strong member of the Party. He appeared to be in charge of the whole hostel. There was one young Jewish doctor, a highly intelligent and intellectual young man who unfortunately was bullied by the other fellows and especially by Emu, who delighted in taunting him after dinner in the evenings. The last night I was there I confronted Emu, telling him that I did not agree with his behaviour and that if this was an example of how Germans were being taught to behave, it was deplorable, and they would never be respected in the world. After arguing for half an hour we retired to bed without a fight. The last evening I was in Hanover I went for a short walk toward the Cafe Krumpke which is in the centre of the city. A very drunk British man was staggering about in front of the cafe shouting at the top of his voice 'F--- Hitler'. He was being followed by two of the Schwarz Corps, 'The Black Guards', Hitler's elite corps, who no doubt soon arrested him.

Hans Brink met me in Berlin and escorted me to a small hotel in Charlotte Strasse which was clean and comfortable but the rooms had only showers and no baths and I do enjoy a bath. The hall porter informed me that there was a good communal bath centre a short distance down the street, so I went to explore. I soon came across quite an imposing building which had a notice outside saying 'Baths – 5 marks'. I went inside but the smell was absolutely terrible and overpowering, so leaving quickly I discovered that I had not read the notice correctly which in fact was 'Dog Bath – 5 marks' — it certainly would have been a new experience for me. I decided to settle for a shower. The next morning Hans escorted me to the Charité Hospital to introduce me to Professor Sauerbuch. Outside the operating theatre he helped me to put on a white gown, cap and mask, then went to dress himself. While waiting for Hans I looked through the operating door, and saw three tables with patients on them, all anaesthetised. Sauerbuch was busily engaged with one and his assistants with the other two. I was feeling rather nervous as I waited for Hans to arrive, then suddenly the calm was broken by Sauerbuch shouting at me: 'Don't stand at the door, either come in or go out'. After Hans had introduced me he became more amenable towards me, but not with his assistants whom he continued to bully. He would also rap their fingers with the back of the scalpel if they didn't pick up the bleeding points quickly.

The following morning I was walking along one of the main streets when I met the extremely small Juanita girl who had travelled on the train with me. She was with a very tall soldier in the Schwarz Corps. She hailed me with a loud 'Hi' and I asked her how she was enjoying Berlin. She replied immensely because she had found a most attractive boy, who unfortunately didn't speak one word of English. The same evening I was with my medical friends having supper in the restaurant of the Wintergarten when above us in the theatre there was great applause and stamping of feet. Juanita and her Girls were performing, Hitler and Goebbels had come to see them.

I spent some very happy days in Berlin with Hans who organised my programme and introduced me to all his friends. His girl friend was a young actress and one of the most beautiful girls I have ever seen. We had a great time together going to concerts and restaurants in the evening. On more than one occasion we went to hear the German State Orchestra with Vorthanger conducting, and Hans knew some of the players. When the weather was good he would call for me in the early morning and take me to a riding school in the forest just outside Berlin, where we could ride through the trees in unspoilt country, and then return to his rooms at the Charité Hospital for breakfast. The stables, where the horses were kept, were part of a large estate which had belonged to a Jewish family who had been forced to leave by the Nazi regime.

I must confess that my stay in Berlin was not very profitable from a surgical point of view. Sauerbuch was all out for speed and drama and he had not the technical ability that I had been used to in London. He was certainly a good cutter but he expected his assistants to stop all the bleeding and if they didn't do so, as I said before, he used to hit them on the back of their hands with a scalpel. When he arrived at the hospital in his black Mercedes, which was lined and upholstered with white Morocco leather, the porter at the entrance gates of the hospital rang a bell, summoning all his staff to the front steps of the hospital building. They formed up in line, clicked their heels together giving him a Nazi salute, saying: 'Good morning Herr Professor'.

My visit was cut short by an event which happened on Friday, November 9th, the so-called Kristallnacht. A third secretary at the German Embassy in Paris, Ernst vom Rath, had been shot by a young Jew. The following day, Saturday, the destruction of Jewish property was encouraged throughout Germany. I went to see what was happening and accompanied a small crowd who were bent on doing as much damage as possible to Jewish shops and synagogues. There were two ringleaders in this particular crowd who were well dressed, in their early twenties, and were carrying ordinary sweeping brooms with which they smashed the Jewish shop windows and swept the contents on to the path and roadway. One of these young men who appeared to be the leader was expensively dressed in a beaver type of coat and a pork pie trilby hat, not exactly as other young Germans could afford to dress. One large crockery shop in an arcade off Friedrich Strasse was devastated. Every bit of porcelain was swept off the shelves until the floor was nearly knee deep in broken pots. After lunch on November 10th Goebbels spoke on the radio and stated that enough damage had been inflicted to express the feeling of the German people for the murder of their Ambassador in Paris. In the afternoon the broken Jewish shops were boarded up, and the Schwarz Corps guarded them. Peace was more or less restored. It seemed too much of a coincidence to me that within little more than an hour of Rohm's murder in Paris hundreds of printed notices were issued and put on doors, lamp-posts and windows saying in large red lettering 'Jewish murderers'. I took down one of these notices and I still possess it. Had this whole show been orchestrated by Goebbels?

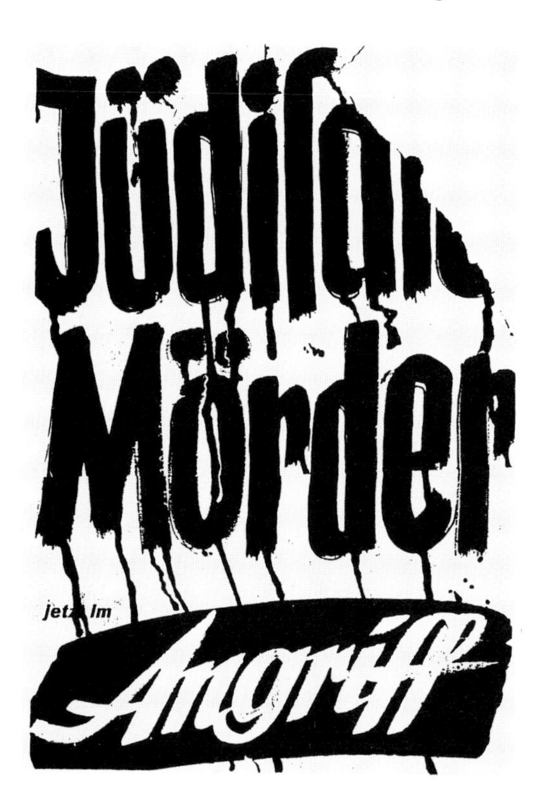

A poster torn down from a Jewish shop, a reminder of Kristallnacht. The reference at the foot is to a propoganda sheet, Angriff (Revenge).

Hans and his friends took me out to dinner in the evening to Zigeuner Restaurant in Charlottenburg which is part of Berlin. After dinner the band played mostly German songs until they were informed that there was an English guest in the restaurant. The band then played *The Lambeth Walk* and I led the singing at our table. After we had finished performing, two of the Schwarz Corps approached our table and requested me to accompany them. Hans came with me because I certainly needed the help of an interpreter. We were escorted to a large building near the Linden. I was accused of stealing from Jewish shops and was thoroughly searched all over to see if they could find anything incriminating. The heels of my shoes were particularly examined to make sure that nothing was hidden inside. Unfortunately, however, I had in my wallet a small document saying that I was a Lieutenant in the Royal Army Medical Corps. After being allowed to dress I was escorted upstairs to a very large room on the first floor. The room was empty except for a table at the far end where an officer was sitting with a large picture of Hitler above his head. He interrogated me for at least an hour. Hans answered the questions, interpreting for me. I had been seen with Hans riding through the forest near Berlin in the early morning. Did I know that this was a military zone and what was a British officer doing there? Hans was also an officer in the German army. He looked uncomfortable for a while, but managed to answer correctly one particular difficult question which appeared to satisfy the German officers. Then finally I was fined fifteen marks and allowed to leave. Hans took me to his rooms at the Charité Hospital and telephoned his chief, Professor Sauerbuch, informing him of what had happened. Sauerbuch told Hans to accommodate me in his own room, and not allow me to go out or return to my hotel. He would come and see me first thing the next morning, so I spent the night on a sofa in Hans' sitting room. The following morning Sauerbuch arrived very early and, after listening to what Hans had to tell him, I was told that I must leave immediately for England. Hans went to my hotel, collected my luggage, paid the bill and returned to me in the hospital. He also booked a seat on the train leaving in the afternoon for Holland. The train would pass through Brunswick at about 8.00 pm, his father, Dr. Brink, who lived there, was requested to meet me at the station and then telephone Hans to say that I had at least reached Brunswick safely. Hans gave me his Nazi badge which I wore behind one of the lapels of my jacket. He advised me to show it if I were accosted by the Police on the journey, and to tell them that I was a follower of Oswald Mosley. I still have that badge. Nothing unforeseen happened, Dr. Brink met the train at Brunswick station, presented me with a packet of sandwiches for the journey, and the train left. I felt a bit uneasy on my own and I must say I

The Nazi badge given to Geoffrey Wooler by Hans Brink.

was quite relieved when we crossed into Holland. When I arrived back in England I went straight to the London Hospital to apply for a job. One of the first people I met was Dr. Dudley Yarrow, a friend from student days who told me I was lucky to get away from Germany because for no reason at all they had recently interned his uncle.

Hans served as a surgeon in the German army throughout the war. His sister wrote to me when the war had finished sadly to say that he had been captured by the Russians at the siege of Stalingrad and that he had died while a prisoner of war of typhus fever.

Hans' father died of a coronary thrombosis soon after the outbreak of hostilities. His mother was a diabetic, and being unable to obtain insulin died in coma. Hans' sister Eva married a lawyer: they live in the Harz mountains and have a family. At Christmas we exchange greetings.

3

The Army Must Sleep on its Stomach

In September, 1938, the Hon. Edgar Hacking had persuaded me to join the Royal Army Medical Corps (Territorial Army) as second Medical Officer to the 1st Battalion the Queen's Westminsters. I thought being second Medical Officer would be an easy job, until a short time later I was informed that a second Battalion was to be recruited, and when the volunteers arrived my responsibility would be to make sure that everyone was physically fit. I spent at least two evenings a week examining new recruits, until we had a full complement of about 1,000 men.

If I remember correctly, I was paid half a guinea for examining each new arrival. After a few weeks I began to feel a rich man because my previous three house surgical appointments at the London Hospital carried no salary, only free board and lodgings.

The medical section on the beach in South Wales.

Lieutenants in the 2nd Battalion, the Queen's Westminsters, at St Donal's Castle, South Wales: (left to right) the Hon Kiwa Plunkett, Frank Lawton, and Denys Rhodes, a descendant of Cecil Rhodes.

Lieut Phillips, Capt & Mrs Anderson, Lieut Bernard Cayzer.

The new recruits were an interesting collection and came from all walks of life. One platoon consisted almost entirely of actors who were members of The Green Room Club in Leicester Square. Fleet Street had provided another platoon, staff from the *Telegraph* and *Mail* being well represented. There were also a few members of the House of Lords, one of whom brought his butler with him to act as batman.

My medical orderly was continually bringing to the medical section large quantities of confectionery for which I was anxious to pay — until I was informed that he was the nephew of the owner of the Lyons Corner House concern.

Col. Savile was the Commanding Officer of the 2nd Battalion. He had had a most distinguished career during the 1st World War, being awarded a D.S.O. with bar and an M.C., when he commanded a battalion of the King's Royal Rifle Corps at the age of 26.

He was a wonderful person, and had a marvellous sense of humour, and we were always great friends.

During the winter of 1939-40 we had a 'flu epidemic. The Assistant Director of Medical Services, who was a regular soldier and had little knowledge of medicine, came to see me and, learning that over half the battalion had a virus infection, asked me if the men were sleeping on their stomachs — about which I had no idea. He told me that if the men did not sleep on their stomachs their privates got cold and they caught influenza; obviously he was thinking of a different way of infection entering the body than I had been taught. I did not argue, he was a full colonel and I a lieutenant.

We were billeted in a school in North London at this time, and rather than keep sick men in army blankets on a classroom floor, with Col. Savile's permission I allowed them to go to their homes, which were all over London.

About 10 days later, the CO became a little disturbed, because when he paraded the battalion only about 150 men turned up on the parade ground, and there should have been nearly 1,000.

He told me that he was expecting a movement order fairly soon, so we must get all the men back as soon as possible, because he had not sufficient personnel even to pack the equipment.

We telephoned and sent cars around London to collect everybody. The response was dramatic, all had recovered and returned to the unit.

After the outbreak of war, the serjeant to the intelligence section of the battalion, who was an actor, was determined to be discharged from the army. He was continually reporting sick, detailing every known hysterical symptom; except he had not yet thought that his head might open and shut. He became a real nuisance and the CO asked me to do all I could to decide how we could handle him. I took him to one of the best psychiatrists in Harley Street, who after examining him, told me that he had always been his mother's darling, and that he should be treated roughly and punished for his behaviour. No mention of the interview in Harley Street appeared on his medical B 178 form. He had seen a civilian specialist, and only the CO and myself knew about this. The CO took his stripes away, and he was reduced to the rank of rifleman. Peace reigned again for a few weeks, and indeed until I took a weekend leave to see my parents. I did not warn the medical officer who stood in for me about the actor. He reported sick again as soon as he saw I was absent. The deputy MO referred him to the Army Hospital at Millbank. He was seen by a young psychiatrist, attended a medical board, and was out of the army before lunch.

When I returned to my unit two days later I was greeted by: 'He's done it, doc'. The sequel to this story is that during 1943 I was in Taranto with the 1st Army and I met in the town a friend from the Queen's Westminsters who used to be a corporal and was now a major. He invited me to dinner in his Mess and after dinner we went to an ENSA show in a cinema.

The film was about the war. The actor who had been a serjeant in the Queen's Westminsters, and discharged for psychiatric reasons, was the hero, winning the war for us. Dressed in full battle order, advancing through a smoke screen, shooting with an automatic Sten gun, he was back in his glory. Nobody in the cinema could understand why we were roaring with laughter — and probably thought we were mad.

September, 1939, we were in Pinner and as we had been at war for just over a month, the Commanding Officer thought it was about time to start training the men. He organised a night operation. In order to test their ability at map reading, they were given only the map references of the route they should follow. The padre and I were told the place where we should assemble the following morning. It was under a railway bridge, so after a few hours' rest the padre and I went in an ambulance to the meeting place, but only the CO and the adjutant arrived — everybody else appeared to be lost: not a good start for what was thought to be one of the best territorial units.

At the time of Dunkirk, all our rifles were taken away and given to another unit to defend London. We were issued with lengths of iron piping with old bayonets welded to one end.

Our men were supposed to be the second line of defence for London, and it was not long before we were all issued with new rifles. After these had arrived the CO ordered a shooting practice, which the padre and I went to see. One of the men insisted on pointing his rifle at least 30 degrees off alignment with the target. He ignored shouts from the serjeant and affirmed he was aiming correctly. The officer in charge ordered the man to come and see me. I found he had weak vision in one eye and a slight squint. He was downgraded medically to prevent him shooting the wrong person.

It was the officers' turn next to have revolver practice, which was carried out on a police range at the rear of Wormwood Scrubs prison.

There was a great mound of earth behind the targets at least 30 feet high and on the top of the mound there were enamelled wrought iron notices advertising Colman's Mustard, Jeyes Fluid etc., increasing the barrier above the targets another four to five feet.

We were issued with .45 Colt revolvers, which are quite heavy and have a considerable kick. One of our young officers was a charming person, but extremely nervous. He started to tremble when it was his turn to hit the target, which had been placed at the bottom of the mound.

While he was standing still, he did manage to fire and hit the mound, but not the target. The second exercise was more demanding, you had to run forward 10 yards and then fire. The young officer after he had completed 10 yards looked to be in a tizzy. We all felt sorry for him but could do nothing about it. His right hand holding the revolver was going round in a circle. The first shot buried itself in the mound, but the second hit one of the iron notices at the top of the mound, ricocheted off the notice and hit the adjutant in the front of his chest, and he was standing next to me. The bullet was spent and did no harm.

This young officer was determined to succeed in the army and eventually overcame his anxiety. In 1944 I had dinner with him in Italy and was delighted to see that he had been awarded an MC, a truly brave and wonderful achievement.

In October 1940 the battalion was sent to Glanusk's Park near Crickhowell in Wales, where we were under canvas. The hall had been leased to the members of the Athenaeum Club in London, who were resident. They had been evacuated for their safety to Wales because they all were very old men in their 80s and 90s. Our officers were made honorary members of the Club, which allowed us to use the main reception rooms in the hall and the bar.

The first night I went into the bar everybody looked dead. The members were all sitting motionless in chairs, and I could not even see them breathe. But not for long, when the bar opened at 6 pm it was like a starter's pistol commencing the 100 yards — everybody suddenly sprang to life, presenting a most active picture. I was relieved, being a doctor, and ordered my gin and tonic.

The Commanding Officer of the Intelligence Section of the Battalion was the Lord Killanin. Just before the outbreak of war he had ordered a pair of Purdy shotguns, tailored to suit him. Before we left London for Wales they were delivered to him.

One Saturday a pheasant shoot was organised in Glanusk's Park and the surrounding estate land. The Lord with his new Purdys was in the first gun position, his butler acting as loader. I was in the second position with a friend, helping him to load. The birds were driven over, hopefully one at a time, Lord Killanin fired both barrels, but the birds just turned their heads and looked at him, wondering why he was making such a noise and was he ill? They flew quietly on until my friend brought them down first shot.

The lord, however, was left handed and fired from the left shoulder, so something needed adjusting and the Purdys were returned.

An interesting character arrived one day at the hospital near to the RAF Station at St. Athans in South Wales, and I got to know him while there to see another patient. He was a Belgian pilot called Alex Nitelet who at the outbreak of War had joined the British Royal Air Force as a flight lieutenant. In early 1940 he was shot down over Belgium and, apart from an injury to his left eye, was unhurt. He disguised himself as a Belgian peasant and managed to reach his own home in Brussels, but it was not for long as his mother insisted that he must return to England to continue to fight. So, after all too short a stay at his home, he left and went via an organised escape route to France and over the Pyrenees into Spain. From Spain it was easy to return to England. He had been examined at the Royal Opthalmic Hospital in London and told that the damaged eye was beyond repair, and should be removed. He was transferred to the Opthalmic Unit at the Royal Air Force Hospital in St. Athans where his eye was removed and then he was downgraded medically and denied the chance to fly again.

After carefully considering his present condition he decided to join the British Secret Service.

They asked him if he would consent to carry messages in an artificial eye which could replace the damaged one and he agreed. A special eye was made which was hollow and one half could be unscrewed from the other to reveal its contents. After the operation he was advised to go to a quiet place in the country to have at least one month's rest. It had to be somewhere where he was not known and would not be recognised. My parents readily agreed to look after him at their house in Shadwell village near to Leeds. A month later he returned to St. Athans in South Wales to be examined by the surgeon. The new eye matched exactly the other one. They moved together and it was quite impossible to tell that it was artificial. The night before departing to a special training unit near to Oxford he gave a dinner party in Cardiff to all his friends. I shall always remember the courteous way he received us at the entrance to the restaurant, thanking us individually and saying that he would be back with us soon. I never heard or saw any more of him. I wrote to his home several times after the War but received no reply. I can only assume he was killed. Perhaps the same fate happened to his mother, if the Germans learned that she had been assisting the Allies.

He was a delightful and charming man who was very brave and one I can never forget.

While in Wales I had been approached several times by my chiefs at the London Hospital saying that I was wasting my time as a Regimental Medical Officer but I knew all the men in the battalion, and now that there was trouble I did not wish to forsake them. Also we all believed that the war would end in less than two years.

However, by December, 1940, many of my friends had left the battalion, most of them being commisioned, so it was beginning to look not quite the same as it had at the outbreak of war.

Mr. Tudor Edwards, for whom I had worked at the London Hospital, was thoracic surgical advisor to all three services, Navy, Army and Air Force, as well as the Emergency Medical Service (EMS). He asked me to dine with him in London. He told me that he wanted me to go to South Wales to look after the chest casualties which were occurring there by the bombing of ports and airfields. I would retain my army rank of captain and be lent to the Emergency Medical Service.

I decided to go, and was glad to be back again in a surgical unit. Also it gave me a chance of reading and renewing my surgical knowledge, which had been denied me as a Regimental Medical Officer. In 1941 I took the final fellowship exam and passed.

Then Hitler decided to attack Russia, the air raids stopped, and there was now no need for me to stay in Wales. So I wrote to Mr. Tudor Edwards explaining the position and asked if I could return to an Army Unit.

In May, 1942, I was transferred as a graded surgeon to the 70th General Hospital stationed in the Examination School in Oxford.

This was quite a new experience for me, because all my patients required something doing below the belt — repairing herniae, treating piles etc. But I was heartened when I remembered what one of my chiefs at the London Hospital had told me — namely, that surgery is only anatomy and common sense. As far as I know I did not make any bad mistakes. The commanding officer of the hospital was a Colonel Whelton, a regular soldier who had served in India, and was extremely knowledgeable in tropical disease, particularly malaria.

One day the medical division admitted a young pilot who was in a coma and had just returned from Africa. He was on the dangerously ill list, and the CO asked me to accompany him to see the patient; within seconds he had diagnosed cerebral malaria, and told me that he was going to prepare some intravenous quinine. About two hours later I was in a cafe opposite the examinations school when I saw a cavalcade of three cars arrive and stop at the entrance to the school. All had flags flying on their radiator caps and everybody who got out of the cars looked like generals. I learnt later what had happened. A delegation had arrived from the War Office to inspect the 70th General, the CO had been informed, but was too engrossed mixing intravenous quinine to remember anything else of importance.

A corporal acting as sentry at the main door let the generals in, and then went to find the CO but he was not in his office and could not be found — so the Orderly Medical Officer appeared and came to greet them. He was Captain David Arnott, who had recently qualified, and looked younger than his age. Unfortunately, he had a terrible stutter which infuriated the generals and made them more impatient than ever. Eventually the CO was found. The generals were not interested in quinine and cerebral malaria so they told him he would be replaced. However, they did not know that the young Capt. Arnott in spite of his stutter had an uncle at the War Office who was Assistant Medical Director. When the generals had retreated, we had to act quickly, and persuaded David Arnott to go immediately to see his uncle in London — which he did the following day. Col. Whelton stayed with the 70th and took it to North Africa with 1st Army. The young R.A.F. pilot with cerebral malaria made a complete recovery thanks to the commanding officer.

Another young soldier who had recently been conscripted was admitted to a medical ward with glycosuria. The physicians were puzzled because all his blood tests were quite normal and the only reason for his glycosuria must have been someone adding sugar to his urine. A thorough search was made of all his possessions. In every army gas mask was attached a small phial containing a de-misting fluid. The phial of this soldier contained sugar. All his possessions were removed for safe keeping, and the next day the staff were pleased because there was no trace of sugar. However, on the following day the urine of every patient in the ward produced a positive sugar reaction, which was both ridiculous and disturbing until it was discovered that sugar had been added to the Fehling's solution, the ingredient used for testing in the ward. In the afternoon the patient's girl friend admitted that she was the culprit and apologised. The soldier was returned to full duty in his unit.

In 1942 Fleming and Florey were producing small amounts of penicillin, and it was fortunate for me at this time because two of my patients were the first to be treated with this new drug. Mrs. Florey would visit in the evenings carrying the precious penicillin in her handbag. On the return trip her handbag was full of bottles containing the patients' urine from which the pencillin had to be extracted. I do not know what the process was, but the extracted and recycled penicillin always smelt of acetone, certainly better than urine.

A young lieutenant, who had just married, went to the Lake District for his honeymoon; and while he was there he developed a boil on the end of his nose. Not wishing to upset his new wife and look ugly — he squeezed it. The infection spread to the veins inside his skull, and when he was admitted to the 70th General Hospital in Oxford, he was in a coma.

Mrs. Florey had another patient at the time and could only spare small doses of penicillin for us. The lieutenant remained in a coma for about a week and we were concerned that he might have developed permanent brain damage. Fortunately, the other patient recovered completely, and then Mrs. Florey was able to let us have about four times as much penicillin, which was immediately given to our patient.

While we were all doing a ward round the following day we saw the lieutenant open his eyes and move his head for the first time. The ward sister at this moment was counting his pulse, and when he saw her more or less holding his hand — his first words were: 'Come, come, sister, my days of frolicking are over, I am a married man'. Obviously no brain damage — the whole ward heard his remark and could not stop laughing.

In October, 1942, we were told to evacuate all the patients from the Examination School and prepare to move abroad. Our injections against different diseases were renewed, and we had a photograph of the complement of the whole hospital taken. After a few days' home leave we had nothing to do except to wait for the movement order, which arrived at our hospital in Oxford on November 8th, 1942.

4
The Explosive Loo

These are extracts from my war diary which I kept daily while I was serving abroad in the First Army from November, 1942 to February, 1946. I am sure nobody wishes to know when it was raining in North Africa, or when it was fine weather and I was able to wash my clothes. All such trivialities I have eliminated. I have related the more interesting times when perhaps I was scared stiff. The bored stiff periods in my original diary remain for my family to read, if they so wish.

Monday Nov. 9th 1942

At 16.30 hours we paraded in full battle order, and marched to the railway station where we entrained. We left Oxford at about 19.00 hours. Next morning we found ourselves in the dock area of Glasgow and boarded the SS *Nea Hellas* which was moored in King George V dock. We were four days waiting in the Firth of Clyde until all the ships in our convoy had arrived.

Sunday Nov. 22nd

We arrived off the harbour of Algiers. We were told to wait as the sea was mined, and we required an escort to guide us through a narrow channel. We thought a French tug was coming to help, but the sailors on board all started gesticulating and shouting at one another, they were obviously not willing to help us at all. Eventually, a British tug arrived and towed us in.

We disembarked after lunch and were given three days' rations and marched East out of Algiers to a small village called Maison Carée where we were billeted in a school.

Wednesday Nov. 25th

After dark there was an air raid warning and we saw flashing lights from a building opposite the school. The lights were of different colours and directed towards the planes. It appeared obvious that someone was signalling to the Germans of our arrival.

Although it was pouring with rain I went with two other officers to Brigade

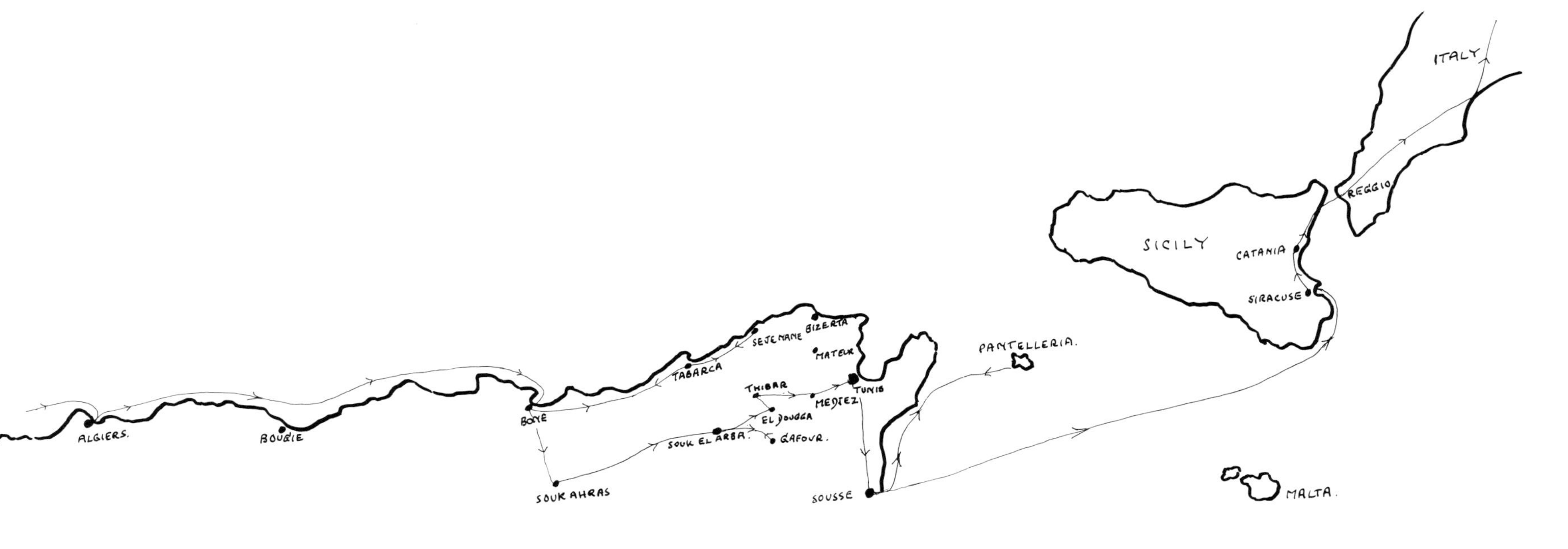

Map of Geoffrey Wooler's movements in North Africa and during the landings on the mainland of Europe.

My Dear Mum Father & Tom

Please address all future correspondence to me as the following

No. 87185 Capt. G. H. Wooler RAMC
70th General Hospital
A.P.O. 4330.

We travelled overnight from Oxford and arrived here in time for breakfast this morning which consisted of bacon and eggs! I slept most of the journey and I went to bed again immediately after breakfast.

I have probably brought too

Hospital whom I know quite well.

I hope Roy enjoys his leave. I spoke to him on the 'phone and he seemed full of the joys of spring.

I have no further news at the moment but will write again when it is possible

Best Love,

Geoff

Geoffrey Wooler's first letter home — censored.

Headquarters to report to their Intelligence Section about the signalling. A corporal came back with us and when he saw the lights he was convinced they were coming from the French Officers' Club. The local gendarmes were informed and they arrested two French officers who were German sympathisers.

Thursday Dec. 10th 1942

Early reveille. Before dawn we all packed our belongings and had a hurried breakfast. We marched to the docks and, after waiting more than three hours, embarked on the *Princess Beatrix*. This was a flat-bottomed fast ship which had been built for use on the Dutch canal system. The *Princess Beatrix* sped East as fast as possible, doing more than twenty six knots, but the vibration was tremendous and continued all night.

Friday Dec. 11th

At dawn 'Action stations' were sounded because a naval officer told us that enemy aircraft had picked us up by dropping flares at about 4.00 am. He comforted us by telling us that ours was the only vessel being escorted by two cruisers and five destroyers. I went up on deck to watch and then the warning 'Any moment now' came from all the ship's loudspeakers at about 7.00 am. The German aircraft approached us singly at a considerable height, flying towards us with the sun. They received a terrific reception from our escorting ships. One plane managed to come low and at about two hundred yards from the *Beatrix*, fired a torpedo. It travelled towards us just below the surface of the water at a great speed. Fortunately, the *Beatrix* was faster than they had anticipated and the torpedo passed astern. There was a short pause and then we were dive-bombed; and we saw two fall forty yards astern of our ship. The attack altogether lasted about an hour and then our fighter aircraft arrived and once more there was peace. During the late morning, we arrived in Bone and camped in a field about a mile from the town.

I was asked to form a small mobile surgical team from the personnel of the 70th General Hospital in order to help the surgeons working with Field Ambulances at the front. I thought it would be a good idea to see what their conditions were like. So on Monday, Feb. 1st, 1943, a Capt. Porterfield from 185 Field Ambulance offered to take me to the front in his car. He had a Dodge 15 cwt. truck with a solid roof covering the front seat from which you could spot planes. We drove all day Eastwards along the main coastal road which eventually goes as far as Bizerta and Tunis, but these towns were still in enemy hands.

After leaving La Calle the road passes through a desolate part of the country. There were many burnt out vehicles dumped by the side of the road and several German tanks in the surrounding fields. In many places the road showed signs of being mined. We arrived at Sedjenane at about 4.00 o'clock in the afternoon. The 185 Field Ambulance was billeted in a tobacco factory along with a number of British and French commandos. About every ten days front line troops came there for forty-eight hours' rest.

I shared a room with the surgeon, Major Gledhill, and his anaesthetist, in a small house adjoining the tobacco factory.

Tuesday Feb. 2nd 1943

We had a quiet night and I slept well, but I hear that Jerry was over and dropped one bomb about a mile away in the woods. After breakfast I went over to see the tunnel in which Gledhill had his Field Surgical Unit. It is safely housed in this railway tunnel and looks as though it would stop anything except a direct hit. The theatre has a wooden and lino floor. There is a resuscitation ward and one other ward with 12 beds adjoining the theatre. They have an ample supply of stretchers. Electric lighting is from a generator or from accumulators. They have also a supply of Tilley lamps. After breakfast I walked through the woods with Col. Pyecroft to inspect the transport lines.

There was almost continuous air activity overhead and an air raid warning sounded at 10 o'clock in the morning and another at 1.00 o'clock in the afternoon. One week previous to our arrival a Jerry plane came over in the afternoon and shot up one of the buildings in the tobacco factory injuring 30 and killing eleven.

In the afternoon I climbed a hill and saw Ball hill in the distance which is held by Jerry. On top of a nearby hill, near to the iron ore mine, there is a French prison which has now been taken over by the Commandos. Two Jerry fighters came over while we were up here and we had to take cover until they had passed. They were not near enough to photograph and passed over without incident.

A mixed French and English commando force is billeted in part of the tobacco factory. Some of the French are very young — in their teens. They go out at night armed with Sten guns to shoot Arabs and anybody they see coming over from the Jerry lines.

The other day, two of them took an Arab out of the village, one of them with a Sten gun and the other carrying a pick and shovel. An hour later they came back without the Arab.

Wednesday Feb. 3rd 1943

Rained a bit in the morning and I wandered around the village. Photographed a Bosch ammunition dump left near the railway.

A unit of Royal Engineers in one of the cottages has an Italian gun which came off a plane. They are repairing it and hope to use it if any planes come over. I thought that a large red cross would be more useful. I photographed the war graves at the back of the factory and also the bombed part of the factory which Jerry visited five weeks ago, when eleven were killed.

Went for a walk in the afternoon on my own, but later met two Medical Officers from the Field Ambulance. Saw two French soldiers setting off for the front, a mule was carrying their kit led by an Arab. They did not wish to be photographed.

A French commando officer arrived in the evening with a two weeks' old scalp wound which is now infected.

At dusk watched the traffic start on the road for the front. All our supplies go up and exchange of personnel takes place at night. I arranged to go up with Captain Porterfield the following night and spend a day at the Advanced Dressing Station and Regimental Aid Posts.

Thursday Feb. 4th 1943

One of the padres of the Field Ambulance wished to go up to the Advanced Dressing Station on a motor bike after breakfast. I was discussing with Gledhill whether it was fairly safe to do this and so avoid a night journey when Jerry planes arrived. We were in our room, Gledhill told me to duck. There was the sound of machine gunfire and cannon. The planes arrived with their engines turned off from the direction of the sun and dived on the tobacco factory shooting with their cannons. There was a colossal roar of engines as they pulled out of their dives and went away. They were quickly followed by a second wave of planes which bombed the factory. I counted at least six bombs which arrived without any whistle. The windows and doors of our room were blown in and both Gledhill and I were covered with glass and wood splinters. My left foot was cut slightly. A crack appeared in the wall above our fireplace, and a grate from the stove shot out through the door, which was difficult to explain.

The whole show lasted about five minutes. I kept to my corner of the room with my tin hat on. The house rocked on two occasions but withstood the racket.

There were signs of machine gunning and cannon fire on the wall of the passage outside our room. A bomb had hit the Main Dressing Station at the other side of the yard to our house, and all the patients in there were killed. An ammunition dump belonging to the commandos in our house was on fire and French commandos were rushing about telling us to get clear because it might blow up any minute.

We took a few necessary things over to the tunnel, while climbing over some railings on the way I tore my trousers. Gledhill soon recovered from this shaking up and started organising things for the reception of casualties.

Several of the Field Ambulance officers came into the tunnel to help. I assisted Gledhill with all the cases — there were twelve. Most of them had multiple injuries so we both worked together in order to get them out of the theatre as quickly as possible.

The batmen brought all our belongings over to the tunnel and at about 3 am we went to bed next to the casualties. L/Cpl. Pitter who was one of Gledhill's staff died just before midnight.

The personnel of the Field Ambulance left the remains of the tobacco factory and took to the hills. They were digging themselves in under bivouac tents when I went to see them in the afternoon, and they were reasonably well hidden under the cork oak trees.

Saturday Feb. 6th

I went over to the tobacco factory after breakfast to empty my bowels. Discovered that our latrine had been fastened up with wire, so undid the wire and found an Arab crouching on the floor. Just then the air raid warning sounded. Did not wish to be caught in the building again so shot out and jumped into the nearest trench. Then remembered the intelligence officer had told me that they had wired up an Arab prisoner in our latrine who had been caught making holes in our petrol tins. When he was asked why he was doing this replied that the Italians were paying him.

While I was in the trench, felt quite sure that the Arab would try to escape and I had not my revolver with me to stop him. But after the planes had passed over I returned to the latrine and the Arab was still there — so I wired him up again myself. Later, informed brigade headquarters about this Arab because in a few days' time he would begin to smell.

I received orders to return to the 70th General Hospital near Bone. The surgeon at an adjoining hospital had been taken ill and I was to do his work. I left in the morning in an ambulance carrying some of the wounded back to a base hospital with me.

Wednesday Feb. 17th 1943

The Commanding Officer came and told me in the evening that I was to pack and go immediately to the 83 General Hospital at La Calle where Killgren their surgical specialist was ill.

I left the 70th after dinner and had a night journey to La Calle in an ambulance. When I arrived I discovered Gledhill and all the staff of the Field Surgical Unit from the bombed factory at Sed Jenane were there as well having a week's rest. He told me that he was moving up to the next tunnel when he returned which is within four miles of the front line; The Royal Engineers are now building two operating theatres for him in this tunnel. If there is an attack in the north he is going to ask for me to go and join him. He told me that a week ago they took in a few casualties from one of our patrols who had been out to lay mines. While they were doing this in Bosch territory a car came along the road with a German officer in and three other ranks. There was a bit of a scrap, because the Bosch had a Tommy gun, and one or two of our men were wounded and had to be left behind. All the Germans were taken prisoner. Two days later one of our men came over to our lines with his arm in plaster, he had been treated by the Bosch at a military hospital near Mateur. He brought a letter to the British brigadier asking what had become of the German officer in the car that had been captured while on patrol, because he was the son of one of their generals. We replied that we had operated on him, and evacuated him to a base hospital in good condition. They returned a message of thanks.

The letter also asked us to tell our pilots to respect the Red Cross because the Bosch had strict orders not to attack it. (Was it at last a gentleman's war?)

Friday Feb. 26th 1943

After arriving at 19 Casualty Clearing Station a message arrived from Corps Headquarters ordering us to prepare all beds, because we were to expect a great number of casualties. They started to arrive in the late afternoon. I operated all the night, stopping once for food at 4.00 o'clock in the morning.

Saturday Feb. 27th

Casualties continued to pour in every four hours. We had three operating tables going in my theatre and I operated and supervised all the day. I had two hours' rest in the late afternoon and then carried on throughout the night until four o'clock. The Commanding Officer of the Casualty Clearing Station, Colonel Pern, kindly assisted me during the night.

Sunday Feb. 28th

Again I operated all the morning and afternoon. Brig. Cantley had been to see me in the morning and had told me to go tomorrow as temporary Officer

Evacuation by ambulance train.

Commanding 31 Field Surgical Unit which is at Gafour because the surgeon, Major Kennedy, was ill with jaundice.

Monday March 1st 1943

At Gafour casualties arrived every night and were mostly men who had been wounded while on patrol. So our routine was to work at night and sleep during the day.

One day a French child was brought by her mother to see me. She had a deep cut of the right index finger which had severed the flexor tendons. The local doctor had sutured only the skin, so the child had no movement of the finger. I performed a tendon suture and, with the aid of penicillin, the wound healed without infection. The child regained excellent movement of the finger. After the war the family sent me a box of dates every Christmas.

Sunday March 21st

I went to morning service at the village church, many French officers were present. Later in the morning Brigs. Cantley and Weddel brought the consulting surgeon to the American armed forces and introduced him to me as Colonel Churchill. He wanted to see a British forward surgical unit. Col. Churchill inspected all my cases in the ward, and then went into the operating theatre to examine the equipment and instruments. He picked up a Doyen lung forceps and asked if I had used them — I answered that I had not so far, which prompted me to enquire whether he was interested in lung surgery, to which he replied that he had tried to study it carefully. I learned later that he was Professor of Surgery at Harvard University, Dean of their Medical School, and a pioneer in thoracic surgery.

Tuesday April 13th

Got up at 05.00 hours before it was light, had a little to eat and then set off in a three ton lorry about 6.30 am. There were about fifteen lorries in the convoy and I was in the seventh vehicle. We went at great speed along the difficult Guardoman road and I lent my sunglasses to the driver because the sun was against us. He skidded around most of the corners and turned the lorry over on one of them. I was bruised a little but nobody was badly hurt. The four men in the back were shaken. It was a narrow escape because fortunately the road was banked at this particular corner and the lorry hit the bank. I continued in another vehicle and arrived at Thibar in the afternoon.

Wednesday April 14th

The 70th General Hospital is under canvas in a field about half a mile from

Thibar village. Got up at dawn and spent the whole day pitching tents and unloading lorries.

A Bosch plane came over in the evening and bombed us — he dropped two 500lb bombs and a number of anti-personnel bombs, which did little damage.

Thibar monastery is situated between the village and our hospital camp site. It was built in the mid-19th century and houses 'Les Pères Blancs' monks. Their toilets have been built over a crevice in the rocks and everything has conveniently disappeared for over a century — until our soldiers arrived.

One man was smoking a cigarette while he used the toilet, and as he got up to dress, he threw the remainder of his cigarette down the toilet and so into the crevice. Immediately there was an ominous rumbling sound, which alerted him, and he left hurriedly before adjusting his clothing.

I was in a field about 200 yards away, when there was a loud explosion like a bomb, and the whole roof of the toilet sailed into the air. Hydrogen sulphide no doubt.

A corrugated iron roof was immediately fitted; but this only lasted two days, when it went up — in spite of a notice on the toilet door: 'No smoking'.

After losing a second roof it was decided not to replace it, as summer was approaching and the weather becoming warmer. Our men were not accustomed to roofs on latrines.

Thursday April 15th 1943

We made a large red cross and I felt safer from air attack.

Wednesday April 21st

At about mid-day Jerry commenced a major offensive and casualties began to pour in. We were the only unit functioning because all the others had packed and were waiting to go forward. Later I learnt that our army had been preparing for a major attack, to force the Germans out of the remaining pocket in Tunisia. He must have received this information and so attacked first.

Thursday April 22nd

The most severely injured of our men arrived during the early morning. They came in hundreds, and many of them died. We had three operating tables going and I worked hard all the day and night. Jerry is attacking in full force and determined to break through our lines. Col. Coyte and Major Owen and many others from the 71st General came to help us.

Friday April 23rd

Wounded continued to pour in the whole day, all very severe injuries.

waiting for our attack 115
wt Tunis

Thursday April 22nd.

The most severe injuries arrived during the early morning. They poured in in hundreds, and many of them died. We had 3 operating tables going and I worked hard all the day & night.

Coyte & Owen and many others from the 71st. general came to help us.

Friday April 23rd.

Wounded continued to pour in the whole day, all very severe injuries.

I had 3 hours rest in the afternoon but otherwise kept going all day & night. Our sisters arrived in the afternoon

Saturday April 24th

We admitted 580 severely wounded cases yesterday.

The 71st. general opened a ward in the next field and

A page from Geoffrey Wooler's diary showing tremendous casualties in the battle for Tunis.

I had three hours' rest in the afternoon but otherwise kept going all day and night. Our nursing sisters arrived in the afternoon.

Saturday April 24th 1943

We admitted 580 severely wounded cases yesterday.

The 71st General opened a ward in the next field and relieved the pressure on us. Also the Casualty Clearing Stations and Field Surgical Units moved forward today. The 50th General arrived and opened in the monastery. I operated until the early hours of the morning and then went to bed.

Sunday April 25th

Got up for lunch. It is Easter Sunday but does not seem a bit like it.

One of the casualties I operated on last night was a young soldier who had sustained an extensive wound to his lower jaw. His mandible had been fractured in three places and part of his tongue was missing. His regimental medical officer at the front had performed a crude tracheotomy which had prevented him from drowning in his own blood and obviously had saved his life. I removed the tube from his trachea and closed the wound. Then I wired his lower jaw to stabilise the fractures, but his tongue presented a problem. A large part of the left side of it was missing showing a raw area of muscle which had to be covered with mucosa. Fortunately, there was a long piece of loose mucosa which was attached only to the tip of his tongue. This strip of mucosa appeared to be ideal for covering the raw muscle of his tongue. When I had finished it I felt quite proud that I had achieved this, but it was not for long. Next morning when I was doing a ward round the young soldier looked at me and said 'What b..... has stitched my tongue to the back of my throat? When is he coming to undo it?' We evacuated him to a general hospital where there was a plastic surgeon. Next morning an American surgical team arrived and were a great help. We are taking in hundreds of casualties a day, some have already been operated on at the forward Casualty Clearing Stations.

Our attack is certainly on but Jerry is harder to crack than I thought.

Saturday May 1st

Spent the day evacuating as many patients as possible. The 71st General took in 980 casualties yesterday and have only six hundred beds.

Thursday May 6th

Our attack for Tunis has started and the air was never free of our planes, relays of bombers escorted by fighters passed overhead all the day long —

making for the direction of Tunis. We took a few minor casualties in during the night but nothing in comparison with the show of a fortnight ago.

Friday May 7th 1943

Planes continued to pass overhead during all the night and day. The men who have come back from the front say that there seemed to be thousands of our planes bombing the enemy.

In the evening we heard that both Tunis and Bizerta fell today at about 4pm.

Monday May 10th

We were told to clear the hospital completely and to expect 2,000 prisoners. All British cases are to go to the 71st General Hospital.

Many more wounded prisoners arrived.

Tuesday May 11th

We took in over 1,200 wounded prisoners today and I was up until 5.00 o'clock in the morning treating them. The Italian and German doctors assisted us.

A notice on the open road heading for Tunis.

Thursday May 13th 1943

The best way of annoying the Bosch is to ask them if they are Italian. They dislike one another intensely.

We allowed the medical prisoners considerable freedom but soon learnt that it was foolish. One night the German doctors burnt our hospital tents saying they have not lost the war, a disgraceful thing to do — so they were taken to a Prisoner of War camp.

Friday May 14th

The ADMS asked me to inspect the wounded left by the Germans in the civilian hospital in Tunis: and to decide whether they all could be evacuated, because we wished to use the hospital ourselves.

To-day we were not busy so after breakfast an officer offered to take me to Tunis in his jeep. We picked up two American doctors on the way. As we passed through what had been the German front line, we counted thirty eight Churchill and Crusader tanks destroyed in a minefield.

Medjez el Bab had been almost completely destroyed and Beja had suffered considerably.

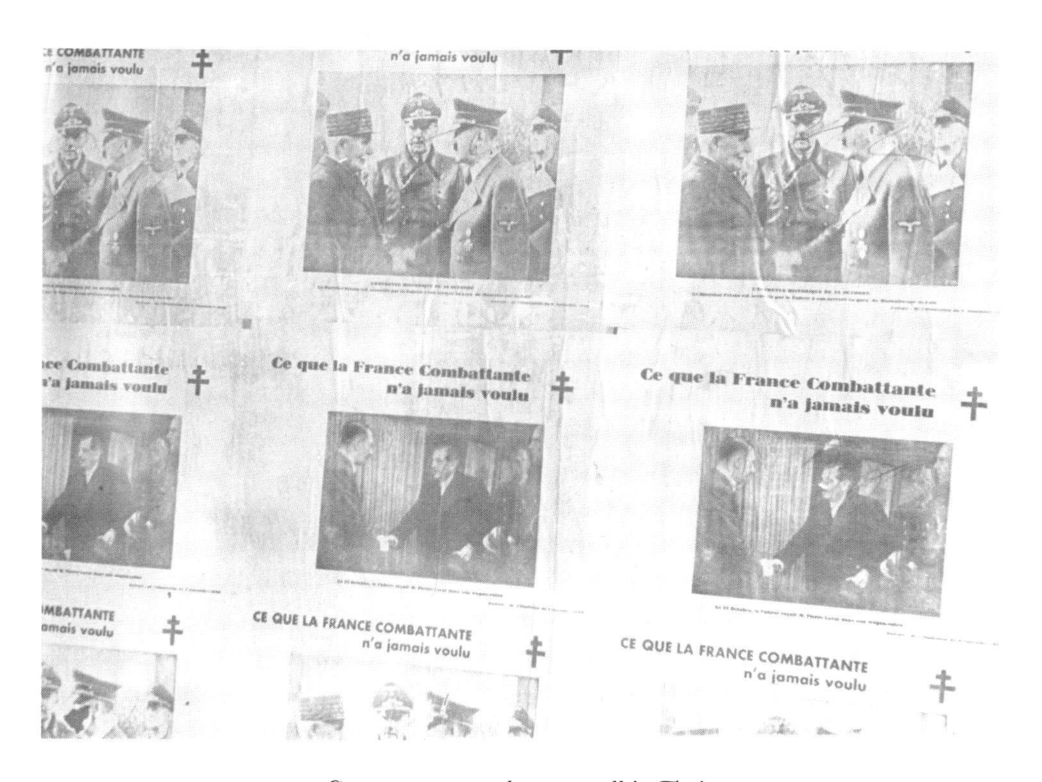

German propoganda on a wall in Tunis.

We had lunch on the sands at Carthage, a delightful residential town built on small hillocks of red sandstone. It faces Tunis bay, where on the other side are high mountains.

I got a lift to Tunis in the Bey of Tunis' car — which was a Citroen. I found my way to the civilian hospital, where two German doctors greeted me and showed me around the wards.

Each ward had that sickly smell of pus and infection. There were only about eight wounded Germans left, presumably because they were considered to be so badly injured that they would not be able to fight again.

One young German had a shell wound of his left thigh with a fractured femur. It was grossly infected and pus was dripping through the bedclothes and mattress into a tin under his bed.

Another had a penetrating wound high up on the front of his chest, also badly infected. When he coughed a spurt of pus flew out and nearly hit me at the foot of his bed.

I told the German doctors that I shall recommend evacuating all these cases either to our base hospitals, or to England where they could receive better treatment. We had penicillin at our disposal, and the Germans had not. The senior doctor gave me his Peugeot car, saying he supposed he would have no further use for it.

The Peugeot car given to Geoffrey Wooler by a German officer.

Capt Mackay and two visiting Americans posing on the facilities at El Dougga near Thiber.

Tunis town is not damaged at all, but the docks and airport have been flattened by our bombing. Eighteen ships in the harbour have been hit and at the airport I was told that there were two hundred and eighty five damaged planes, only six of which could be made serviceable.

It was becoming dark so I left Tunis in the Peugeot and drove back to Thibar by myself during the night.

Saturday May 15th 1943

Back at the 70th General in Thibar, German sick and casualties continued to arrive in their hundreds. They believe that we are going to fight with them against Russia after the war.

Thursday May 20th

Victory day in Tunis. The American surgical team left at an early hour to fly over Tunis in the victory demonstration.

5
Fleas, Flies and Faeces

Wednesday, June 9th 1943

With the war over in Africa, the Allies turned their attention to Europe. I was given full information about the forthcoming operation. We are going to take Pantelleria if they do not decide to surrender, and I am to go with the No.3 Field Surgical Unit in an invasion barge and land one and a half hours after zero hour on the island. I am replacing their Officer Commanding, Major Rogers, who is ill in 71 General Hospital. Capt. Toland — his anaesthetist — and I went to see him in the evening. They are not sure whether he has appendicitis or colitis.

Thursday June 10th

We are to take the absolute minimum with us. I was issued with an entrenching tool, and I changed into denims for I thought they would be more serviceable than tropical kit.

To:- Capt. G.H.Wooler, R.A.M.C.,

From:- O.C.,70th General Hospital,

You will be ready to move at 14.00 hrs., today, 9th June,1943.

You will carry battle order, one pair of long trousers and bed roll.

Transport will be at the Hospital at 14.00 hrs.

Major.R.A.M.C.,

9th JUNE.43. Registrar for, O.C.,70th General Hospital.

Order received by Geoffrey Wooler for the invasion of Pantelleria.

The landing craft which took Geoffrey Wooler to land on Pantalleria.

Called to see Major Rogers on the way, he is certainly not fit to come and his appendix is going to be removed.

After a midday sandwich we went to an assembly area near Sousse where the whole brigade collected, and after a rest and a cup of tea we went to Sousse docks, and embarked on a new type of invasion boat built by the Yanks which has never been used before. These landing craft are being tried to see if they will be suitable for the invasion of France. The Main Dressing Station, Field Surgical Unit, Field Transfusion Unit and brigade headquarters are on board so it is rather an important cargo. I am on two deck with three other medical officers and fifty four other ranks. We have a wooden armchair each, which are not too comfortable.

After dark Jerry came over and bombed us while we were at anchor in Sousse bay. A terrific barrage was thrown up and metal clattered on to the decks. Our ship was hit and damaged so we had to change on to another in the bay.

We left Sousse about midnight and had no further disturbances.

Friday June 11th 1943

Just after dawn we sighted Cape Bon and sailed past it escorted by aircraft and destroyers. There were 24 ships in the convoy including the *Princess Beatrix*, her sister ship, and the *Ulsterman*.

After breakfast we sighted 18 invasion barges loaded with tanks and beyond them in the distance we saw Pantelleria.

Flights of American Bostons passed overhead every quarter of an hour and bombed the town.

The navy commenced its bombardment at 11 am. I could see one cruiser firing and saw its shells bursting on the island. At this time three fast motor boats passed us and we were told that they were going to rush through the harbour boom. Troops were climbing down into small landing craft from the larger ships at the same time.

While the naval bombardment was on 120 bombers dropped their load and the whole island disappeared from view in smoke. At noon, Pantelleria has surrendered, and everybody is very happy.

At 1 pm, I saw a nearby cruiser being bombed but could not get my camera ready in time. Photographed the cruiser just afterwards, it appeared to be undamaged which was fortunate because General Eisenhower and Admiral Cunningham were on board.

We are now going straight for the harbour, and while we were docking a number of American aircraft came over and bombed the island. I saw the bombs drop and explode, it marked the commencement of phase two of the original plan. The pilots evidently did not know that the island had surrendered.

Storage tunnels for oil at Pantelleria harbour where Geoffrey Wooler operated amid fleas, flies and faeces.

The whole town is one mass of ruins and not one house is habitable. All the roads are damaged and the main road out of the town impassable. I have never seen so much destruction anywhere.

We waited on the quayside for a while and then were ordered off. American newsreelmen and reporters were rushing about taking photos, one of them informed me that we were the first to land in Europe. We unloaded our equipment and then each carried a large box through the remains of the docks. The box Toland and I were carrying was much too heavy and we asked two Italian prisoners to take it for us.

We are billeted by the side of the docks in a petrol store which has never been used as such. It consists of tunnels and rooms hewn out of the rock. The Italians have been using the place as a first aid post and it is full of refugees, casualties, furniture, fleas, flies and faeces.

Their medical inspection room needed a lot of cleaning. It was full of junk but we managed to set up our equipment and were ready to receive wounded within two hours. Jerry visited us in the evening and dropped a few bombs in the harbour. I had operated on five casualties but they were not serious.

Saturday June 12th 1943

I slept in the open last night but did not have much rest. The place smells of faeces. I was bitten by fleas, barked at by a dog and an Italian nearly defaecated on me. The whole place is lousy with dysentery. We had two dive bombing attacks by Jerry during the day and one or two fell rather close but he was quickly driven off by our Spitfires.

Sunday June 13th

Not a bit like Whitsunday. The island is volcanic and little or no vegetation on it. Breakfast consisted of a slice of bully and a few biscuits — afterwards I deflead myself and caught eighteen. I was bitten all over and could feel them moving about. I had to take off my clothes and deflea myself at least twice a day. I became quite professional at catching them.

We were told to move the theatre in the afternoon to the other side of the island into the Italian naval hospital at Khamma. Jerry made three divebombing attacks on the harbour during the day and one bomb fell next to the Main Dressing Station — a wooden structure fell on to a number of our beds which were in the open, fortunately they were unoccupied.

All Italian medical personnel and their sick on the island are to be evacuated by boat. The bombing upset them considerably while they were being loaded on to the ships. Later, while we were packing the theatre, a gunshot wound of the abdomen arrived. I operated on him and was a bit distracted by the fleas and filth, then sent him off straight away to Khamma. Just after him Group Capt. Atcherley, a member of a York family, arrived with a head wound and a compound right radius and ulna. After operating on him, I sent him off as well to get him away from the appalling conditions where we had to work.

He commanded a Beaufighter squadron stationed near Cairo. Without permission he had flown over to Pantelleria to see the first bit of Europe captured by the Allies. The airstrip at Pantelleria was full of bomb craters which severely damaged his plane and put it out of commission.

In the underground hangar he selected a small Italian observation plane which had only one engine. Whilst attempting to start this engine it backfired, and caused the injury which brought him to my surgical unit.

Later in the day we packed everything on to a small Italian truck, climbed on top of the boxes and set off.

The road led around the coast where we saw some signs of vegetation. There were many bomb craters on the road, some were filled in, others we had to drive around off the road. The truck had a puncture near Khamma, so Toland and I walked on and left it.

The island here is more attractive, there is a little surface soil: vines and fig trees managing to grow.

The Italian marine hospital is about half a mile from the village and consists of about seven converted houses. It has been left in a filthy state but outside it looks an attractive building. I walked around the village, got rid of another four fleas and then went to bed in one of the wards.

Monday June 14th 1943

Slept very well last night without clothes and rolled up in one blanket on a mattress. Most comfortable night I have had since leaving Sousse.

Went around the billets in the morning. The Italians are taking over the civilian hospital in the village, and are going to run it themselves.

Visited the aerodrome and inspected the underground hospital which is lavishly equipped.

Also was shown the underground hangars which must be a quarter of a mile long into a mountain. Planes, cars, small tanks, clothing and equipment have been left in good condition. I brought a few things back with me including a typewriter. There were three unexploded bombs which we had to pass to get to the hangars, and we had to dive for it when returning for there was another divebombing attack. I grazed my arm and leg again.

Returning to the hospital, met Major Parker there who is to take over from us tomorrow. A number of bomb casualties arrived and I was busy operating until the late evening. The villagers brought us some wine, and we had a small party with two Italian naval M.Os.

Tuesday June 15th 1943

Did not sleep well last night, and was rather cold on a stretcher with only one blanket.

We are leaving the hospital this evening, No.2 Field Ambulance and their Field Surgical Unit are taking over. Atcherley, who is recovering well, is trying to arrange for a Hudson bomber to come from Tunisia and collect him. I am awaiting its arrival now, for he wants to take me back to Tunis with him. The bomber arrived, but considered it too dangerous to attempt a landing, so returned to Tunis.

Major Parker arrived about midday and I showed him around the hospital and my cases. In the evening I joined my Field Surgical Unit at an assembly area about two miles from the docks. We parked in a field by the seashore. One of the unit's men found a pair of German field glasses.

We are very near a battery of Italian coastal guns, they are in caves hewn out of rock rising up 100 ft from the sea, quite impregnable. These caves are also full of fleas so we did not explore them.

We all had a bathe which was not easy because we had to climb over rocks in our bare feet.

The Main Dressing Station had been given a barrel of wine by the villagers of Khamma and we drank this in the evening: then we went to bed and were devoured by mosquitos.

Wednesday June 16th

There was a very short raid during the night, and one yesterday evening which I photographed. Breakfast consisted of bully and biscuits, after which the Italian lorries took our packs and equipment to the docks. We passed many American soldiers marching inland as we made our way to the harbour. Major O'Neill with his section from the Field Ambulance caught us up on the way and we marched down to the harbour and went on board two Landing Craft Infantry which were waiting.

We left Pantelleria at 11.30 hrs just at the time Jerry used to come and divebomb the harbour. But fortunately he was late today and we cracked out as fast as possible into the open sea. Another Landing Craft Infantry accompanied us and together we came back by an Easterly and more Southerly route unescorted. We passed a destroyer of the Hunt class just off Pantelleria and later a convoy of tank landing craft going towards the island. The walking wounded cases were on board with us including Atcherley. They all took the journey well in spite of the heavy sea. Group Capt. Atcherley kept us amused on board the landing craft which helped a lot, because outside was a bit noisy. He was dressed in pyjamas, a silk dressing gown and carried a 'fly whisk'.

I was in an Italian naval rating fatigue kit which I had found at the naval hospital, it was at least clean. I had discarded my own clothes because they were filthy and stained with my own blood from the bites I had received.

The two Italian garments — trousers and a shirt — puzzled me, they were unusual because they were secured by lacing at the back, rather like Victorian corsets: or, was I wearing them back to front? In that case I could not use the four pockets, because they would all be in the rear.

We arrived back in Sousse at about 10.00 pm without an escort. After disembarking Atcherley and I immediately went and sat at the front of a waiting ambulance. We were accosted by a young efficient naval officer who was in charge of the transport and evacuation from the ships.

He swore at us, and ordered us out of the ambulance. Fortunately, Atcherley had brought his service cap with him which was somewhere under his dressing

Back in North Africa at Sousse in an Italian deck-hand's kit.

gown. He put it on with its two rows of gold oak leaves and turning to the naval officer he said, 'Allow me to introduce you to Major Wooler', and I, looking like a Billingsgate porter, said, 'I wish to introduce you to Group Captain Atcherley'.

The navy apologised and gave us the best salute I have ever had — being accustomed to the R.A.M.C. I took Atcherley to the 71st General Hospital where we had supper together and then I returned to the 70th and slept the night in ward 1.

Saturday June 26th 1943

Brigadier Lionel Whitby, General Poole and a Colonel arrived. They had arranged a conference of all the Field Transfusion Units at our hospital. I showed Brig. Whitby photographs I had taken and he agreed to take them back to England with him in his diplomatic bag but he had to visit Cairo first before returning to London. I was grateful about this as I thought it was a secure way of disposing of them.

Saturday July 10th

The invasion of Sicily commenced at 3.00 o'clock to-day. We were told to expect casualties about noon on Monday. I went for a swim in the afternoon.

Sunday July 11th

The first casualties arrived in the afternoon. They came back in the Princess Beatrix and were all very minor injuries. I finished my cases before midnight.

There were several Canadians and Americans amongst the casualties. One patient called Cross lives in Acomb near York.

Thursday July 22nd

I was surgeon on duty. We took in a few cases but nothing very exciting. The consulting malarialogist to the Army who was a Brigadier General arrived with his adjutant — a Colonel — I was introduced, but forgot their names. They had come to see Col. Whelton, our CO, whom they knew was interested in tropical diseases. I was invited to lunch with them in our mess. Our guests asked for a glass of water. Now we kept our drinking water in unglazed earthenware chatties. The water can pass through the pores of the chatty, evaporate and cool the contents in the pot — by the so-called latent heat of steam. Nobody drank water in our mess and the chatties had been neglected and left uncovered for some days. A mess orderly arrived at our table with a jug of water and filled the glasses of our two visitors; which could not have caused more surprise and excitement. At first I wondered why there was suddenly a deathly silence and why our visitors were carefully examining their glasses before drinking — the Colonel spoke first: 'Good God the anopheles mosquito', then the Brig. Gen. said: 'By jove, I've got a pupa'.

Fortunately they took it in good part, joked about it, and ordered some beer.

Sunday Aug. 8th 1943

I am Orderly Medical Officer and went to morning service which was a combined effort by two padres, Captains Tyson and Whittingham: the latter prayed that the next hospital site would be better than the present one. It could hardly be worse. Had tea in the sisters' mess.

We received orders to move to Sicily. As I was mess secretary, after obtaining permission, I decided to give a farewell party to the sisters and medical officers of all the R.A.M.C units in the Sousse area.

In the afternoon one of the young medical officers in No. 1 Field Amb. came to see me, and pointed out that the sisters would be grossly outnumbered by the officers at the party. His fellow officers had wagered him that if he dressed and disguised himself as a nursing sister he would not obtain a dance. I did not object.

In the evening I was at the entrance to the entertainment tent receiving our guests and introducing them to one another when one of my friends stopped and said to me, 'Geoffrey, you have the most extraordinary nursing sisters attending

Mural from Luftwaffe headquarters, Catania, Sicily — Stalin asking for help and Roosevelt in doubt.

tonight, because I have seen one, standing up, and relieving herself into a cactus plant'. I replied that everything was possible in the 70th Gen. Hospital.

The young officer did obtain a dance and did win his wager. I am not sure what happened afterwards but several hefty medical officers pursued him out of the tent.

Tuesday Aug. 10th 1943

We are on the hospital ship *St. David* sailing towards Sicily. Got up at about 7 am just as we were passing Cape Pessano. We passed a convoy sailing up the East coast of Sicily. We kept out at sea well away from the coast and from all other shipping.

Had breakfast and then we passed Syracuse and Fort Augusta. Mt. Etna appeared pencilled out in the haze. About midday we came inshore to Catania at the foot of Etna, and after lunch and saying goodbye to the staff of the *St. David* we went in an ambulance to 15 Casualty Clearing Station.

Wednesday Aug. 18th

Having arrived in Catania four days ago with no direct orders as to the building where we should unpack our equipment, it was finally decided at a conference yesterday that we are to move into the new barracks which are not quite finished but they offer extensive floor space and seem to be ideal for a hospital.

Monday Aug. 30th

Captain Thompson, my anaethetist, and I found a German parachute made of silk. An Italian offered to make a pair of pyjamas each from it. She charged us equivalent to ls 6d per pair, but when we tried them on we found they were transparent — alright if you are married, but we weren't.

Saturday Sept. 11th

Very busy in the hospital. I took in fifty six casualties which had been badly treated by 8th Army surgeons further forward.

The problem with 8th Army surgeons is that they have been treating injuries in the desert where there is not a lot of infection. They do not perform a full wound excision as we have been doing in the 1st Army but just a slight trimming — this doesn't work when there is manure in the soil. All the wounds I saw treated by 8th Army surgeons required further surgery — a much wider excision and opening up of the deep fascia to relieve tension. This difference in surgery caused a certain amount of friction between the consulting surgeon to the 8th Army and the consultant to the 1st Army when they first met in Tunisia.

6

War in Italy — Insects Galore

Saturday Sept. 25th 1943

With Capt. Thompson we left Catania airport at 9.30 am in an American transport plane which is not very comfortable. Flew along the Eastern coast of Sicily and then up the Western coast of the toe of Italy. We cut inland and stopped for about half an hour at advanced R.A.F. H.Q. The plane, greatly reduced in weight, took off again and cut across the bay to Taranto. We arrived at Taranto airport about noon and one of the paratroop Jeeps took us to their Field Ambulance whose building we are taking over. They are in a T.B. sanatorium about two miles the other side of the town.

Monday Sept. 27th

When we arrived at the T.B. hospital near Taranto the building looked wonderful. A nun dressed in yards of flowing white material met us and escorted Tommy and me to a double room which had a balcony overlooking some pine trees in the garden.

Two beds were already prepared with white sheets and counterpanes, what apparent luxury! We went downstairs to explore, met the others of our advance party, then went to have a meal in the dining room. A soldier asked us to inspect the kitchen, which presented a horrifying sight, we had never seen anything like it before. Every wall and the whole ceiling were covered with cockroaches — there must have been millions. They were even on the doors, so that when you turned the knob to go out, some fell up your sleeve. We were all very tired, so we ate the rations we had brought with us and retired to sleep. I had had experience of Italian hospitality in Pantelleria. I pulled my bed to bits and inspected the mattress. Around the seams there was considerable evidence of dead bed bugs which for want of anything else had eaten one another.

Tommy could not believe me when I told him that I was going to sleep on the balcony with the one blanket I had carried with me and my gas mask as a pillow. Tommy changed into his pyjamas, got into bed, and I was soon asleep

Map of Italy showing Geoffrey Wooler's movements.

on the balcony: but not for long. About two hours later he awoke me with his torch. He was covered with bed bugs, all as flat as wafers, and they seldom had been so lucky. He removed his clothes and we knocked off all the bugs from his body, but he was without clothing to put on, and I being the senior officer, did not want him on the balcony. However, eventually we came to a compromise, I moved to one end of the balcony and he slept at the other.

The main aqueduct supplying southern Italy had been destroyed so there was no water supply to the hospital, and no toilet was usable because every one was full to the brim with haemorrhagic dysenteric excreta. Also outside in the garden, under the pine trees nearest to the building, the ground was contaminated all over with haemorrhagic stools. The sanatorium from a distance looked an attractive building, but we, in the advance party, decided we could not use it until it was cleaned. How the paratroop Field Ambulance and a Field Surgical Unit had managed before our arrival I do not know.

We chose a site in a field a few hundred yards away to pitch out tents when they arrived, but this proved unnecessary for a gang of our pioneer corps got to work and within a few days the sanatorium was reasonably clean. So when the 70th General arrived one week later they were able to use the building.

Wednesday Oct. 27th 1943

A paratroop padre came to see me last week-end. He had been over to Yugoslavia in a destroyer and had been brought back in a captured German merchant vessel. He informed us that three hundred Yugoslav patients are due to arrive at 11.30 pm tonight from Bari, but most of them are fit enough to be evacuated by hospital ship tomorrow.

Friday Nov. 26th

Felt ill when I got up. Operated throughout the morning sitting on a large pad of cotton wool much to the theatre orderlies' amusement. Went to bed before lunch feeling really very ill — aching all over and shivering. Both Captain Stevens and Colonel Lee Lauder saw me and I was sent to the officers' ward.

Saturday Dec. 4th

I have been in bed now eight days and am feeling much better. I have infective hepatitis and am slowing turning a yellowish green colour, my eyes are yellow and I noticed that my urine has been dark for the past two days. My posting to 26 Field Service Unit came through last Tuesday from the Headquarters of Allied Forces but no date was specified, so Major Wicks, the Company adjutant, wrote to ask about this.

Jerry had a lucky raid on Bari last Thursday night which caused massive destruction to our shipping. His first flare fired an oil tanker, then he dropped a stick of bombs which blew up an ammunition ship. Altogether ten ships were burnt and seven others damaged. They were docked too closely side by side and fire spread from one to the next. Our fire lorry went to help — but I do not know what use it could be.

The 98th General Hospital in Bari took in three hundred casualties and we admitted about fifty from a destroyer yesterday. I helped with the casualties even though I was still very weak. The raid on Bari harbour had been very destructive. The other hospitals in Bari were soon filled, the overflow of casualties arrived at the 70th General Hospital during the night.

The ones that came to us were caused by our own mustard gas, carried on one of our ships which was hit. This was a closely guarded secret. Not even the crews of the ships carrying the gas knew about it. Certainly in this theatre of war nobody was informed until the following day, when an official flew over from the War Office in London and gave us the terrible news. Tragically this was too late, because we did not know the true cause, and nearly all the cases we admitted died. I saw casts of the bronchial and tracheal mucosa being coughed up, having been destroyed by the gas. Patients were given intravenous saline and plasma with no beneficial effect.

But in the Bari hospitals most of the men had been wounded. They were washed and bathed in order to clean their wounds before surgery: and most of these cases recovered. The washing and bathing had removed the mustard gas from their skin. The cases we received in Taranto had not been wounded, and had we known the cause, and washed them when they arrived, we could have saved many lives.

Thursday Dec. 9th 1943

I am still yellow but am feeling very much better and my appetite has returned.

Two days ago Col. Anderton, assistant director of medical services with the 1st Division, came to see me, having just arrived from North Africa. Since Pantelleria, they have been engaged in mountain warfare and their field ambulances have been issued with mule stretchers. He told me to be well within five weeks because there is another show on, a landing at Anzio.

Tuesday Dec. 14th

A telegram arrived today from headquarters stating that I am to exchange positions with Major Latchmore who is Officer Commanding 26 Field Service Unit and I should receive my majority. I immediately wrote and told my parents.

Wednesday Dec. 15th 1943

The hospital is quiet, so although I am still a patient and convalescing from jaundice I volunteered to act as orderly medical officer in the evening and allow most of the staff to go out together.

Soon after dark one of the nursing sisters came to see me and informed me that she was unable to control a dispatch rider who had a head injury and could not speak. Last night and tonight he had left his room, then gone into the general ward and removed all his clothes. Nobody could restrain him, he refused to go back to bed and the sister thought he was a mental case. After being informed that he was in the same room that Tommy and I had occupied when we first arrived in Taranto, I told the sister that perhaps he was more intelligent than they imagined. We went to his room pulled the bed to bits, it was the same one which previously had been alloted to me, and there were the bugs, not many, but now they were blown up like small balloons with blood. They are more easily crushed in this condition, but it makes a mess.

Sunday Dec. 19th

Major Latchmore arrived in the evening from San Severo to take over from me, so I shall have to leave within a few days. I am to join a Canadian casualty clearing station which is moving forward very soon.

Tuesday Dec. 21st

The CO gave a farewell dinner party to me in the evening and toasted my health. I replied and thanked them for all the help they had given me. I was sorry in many ways to be leaving.

Wednesday Dec. 22nd

Breakfast at 5.00 am with O'Neill who later boarded a ship at Taranto for England. We left the 70th at about 6.15 am when it was just becoming light, and we went up the Bari road as far as Gioia. Then Westwards over the Apennines through Altamura and Potenza to the Salerno plain where the two towns of Battipaglia and Pontecagnano are almost completely destroyed. We arrived in Salerno just as it was becoming dark and I stayed at the Hotel Diana.

Thursday Dec. 23rd

We took the main road to Naples, all the bridges had been blown and considerable lengths of the road had been mined. The road passed through some of the best orange groves I have ever seen, large trees laden with fruit. There were many refugees on the road, women carrying large parcels of all their possessions on their heads and we were asked innumerable times to give lifts.

Before leaving Salerno we had to go to the back of the town to fill up with petrol. Here we saw many desolate people living in bombed buildings under the most appalling conditions. The filthiest Europeans I have ever seen came out of these destroyed buildings, women without shoes or stockings, wearing little clothing and hair all over their faces. They hardly looked human. They clustered around the car obviously wanting food, but we were forbidden by the army to give them any. In fact we had very little to give them.

We saw Vesuvius which had a cloud on top, and Capri. I stopped for about an hour in Pompei to look around the ruins. The main street of the old town had been bombed, and some of the ancient Roman houses which have taken years to dig out have been damaged.

Friday Dec. 24th 1943

We drove from Naples to the Foggia plain and at dusk arrived in the small town of Torremaggiore, where we are attached to No. 4 Canadian C.C.S.

Saturday Dec. 25th

Christmas Day in Torremaggiore pouring with rain and cold, but we are in a building with a cheery lot of Canadians and have plenty of food. We are billeted in the village school and are really quite comfortable.

At 10.00 am I went to morning service followed by Holy Communion. Noon was the men's dinner at which the officers served the men. Our dinner was at 6.30 pm. American and British officers were asked to come as guests. Various toasts were proposed after the meal, including our own, to which I replied by toasting Canada.

7
Cassino Battle

Thursday Feb. 17th 1944

A British major arrived with two Russian officers in the afternoon. They had come over from Yugoslavia by submarine and as they were both surgeons, they wanted to see a forward British surgical unit.

The major was obviously 8th Army, wearing a brightly coloured scarf around his neck, polo boots, riding breeches, no cap and a monocle. I was informed that he was an exceedingly brave man and had been parachuted into almost every country in Europe. His technique was to take his monocle out just before he jumped, then after a safe landing put the monocle back and walk on. I know this because one of my friends went with him to Yugoslavia.

The two Russians were both colonels and they brought their batmen with them, who seemed to act as bodyguards as well, standing behind them and serving them in the mess. At dinner they wore full mess uniform with gold braid, medals etc. not exactly my idea of communism, for in comparison we had to serve ourselves, and always wore battledress on active service.

The Russians were not in favour of general anaesthesia. They preferred local and told me that if you blow up a damaged limb with lots and lots of saline beneath the deep fascia until it is like a drum — it provides sufficient anaesthesia for a quick amputation. A method I would not care to try. They stayed only one night and left after breakfast to see a general hospital.

Friday Feb. 25th

We crossed over to the other side of Italy north of Naples. It is not difficult to see that the Americans had been here before us because most of the local farmers and their children are going about in American uniforms.

Monday Feb. 28th and Tuesday Feb. 29th

There was a surgical conference at 1st New Zealand Casualty Clearing Station. A very old Col. Stout, their consulting surgeon, presided. The New Zealanders say that he is too old to return to his home.

Wednesday March 8th 1944

We packed our equipment and moved after breakfast to 1st New Zealand Casualty Clearing Station. The light section of No. 7th British Casualty Clearing Station came with us, making three surgical teams in readiness for when the battle for Cassino commences.

Thursday March 9th

The New Zealand Corps attack to take Cassino has not yet begun.

To-day, an American bathing unit arrived and installed itself in a nearby field. We have been invited to use it, so in the morning I went there with Alan Hollinrake, my anaesthetist. The unit is made of three large communicating tents. In the first you strip completely and hand in all your clothes, then you climb a staircase in the second tent where you are given a tablet of soap, you go slowly through a series of 12 showers starting with a tepid one, increasing in temperature to about as much as you can tolerate, then the showers gradually cool until the final one is quite cold. I felt happier in the cold one. You then descend some stairs, are given a large towel and enter a warm drying tent. Hot chocolate is served and there are plenty of magazines and newspapers to read.

If you are American, you are issued with a complete set of clean clothing, but being British my old things were handed back to me — and I really felt most uncomfortable. I had never been so clean since I left England, and it took me a few days to get used to it.

In the afternoon I sent all the men to have a bath.

Our operating theatre is ready for action.

Wednesday March 15th

The Battle for Cassino by New Zealand corps began. Bombers roared overhead during the morning and we could hear their loads bursting. A few casualties arrived in the afternoon, caused mostly by our own bombing. Attack headquarters was hit and Gen. Leash's kitchen and caravan knocked about.

Wednesday March 22nd

Jerry planes visited us during lunch hour and I saw two brought down. Jerry is still holding on to Cassino. We are told to prepare for heavy casualties.

Thursday March 23rd

We were busy operating all day, but were not called during the night. Vesuvius is in action and I saw smoke arising to a very great height over Naples.

Wedneday March 29th 1944

The New Zealand Corps has suffered heavy losses and succeeded in taking only the railway station at Cassino. It has failed to capture the town, so the Corps has been dissolved and the 13th British Corps has taken over.

Wednesday April 5th

We were informed by 13 Corps that we are to move forward on Friday to the 'Inferno Valley' near Cassino. At 17.00 hours on Friday, at a place called San Michele, we shall meet a guide who will escort us the remainder of the way to the valley.

Friday April 7th

I decided to take one Bedford three-tonner and the Dodge truck. We left 7 Casualty Clearing Station after lunch. The Bedford broke down at S. Vittore and again at Cervaro. From there onwards we were under direct observation of the Bosch. We could plainly see the monastery, and Cassino in the valley. For about two to three miles from San Michele onwards we were within mortar

French North African troops, who had a fearsome reputation, passing down Inferno Valley. The tents are part of a field hospital.

range, but the Germans respected our red crosses and we had no trouble and heard no noise.

We arrived at the Main Dressing Station of the 11th Field Ambulance in the late evening. They are in the 'Inferno Valley', about three miles from Cassino. We are taking over from Major Milne who is in charge of 28 Field Surgical Unit. He wanted to exchange tents and I was not surprised when I saw his because they were so old. I refused and sent Evans back with an ambulance to 7 Casualty Clearing Station to collect mine. Milne was not a bit pleased.

Captain Sutton is also here with 26 Field Transfusion Unit. Several shells fell quite close during the night and I sheltered in Sutton's tent which is well dug in.

Saturday April 8th 1944

On the latrines I was surprised to find myself in full view of Mt. Cairo, the Bosch main observation post, and I wondered if they could see me. Driver Evans arrived back after lunch and we put up our tents.

Sunday April 9th

Very noisy last night. Shells whizzing overhead in both directions but nothing fell close. We have pitched our operating tent on the side of the hill and can plainly see Mt. Cairo from it, which is the main German observation post. The American ambulance drivers are next to us.

My whole surgical unit slept last night in the operating tent, I was fortunate to have a stretcher. I was awakened in the early morning by one of my men saying 'We are one extra' then a moment later he said 'Coo'er he's a stiff'.

Somebody had brought a dead casualty back during the night on a stretcher, and pushed him under a wall of our operating tent.

Tuesday April 11th

A lot of shelling during last night.

Was awakened at dawn by a loud explosion which shook the tent and covered it with earth. I thought it was the Royal Engineers blasting but discovered that a shell or mortar had landed about 30yds from our tent — two trees had been uprooted but nobody injured.

Monday April 17th

I was up most of the night dealing with some extensive abdominal injuries.

Harold Rogers, now a Colonel, assisted me. He and Colonel Poole Wilson left after breakfast with four abdominal cases in an ambulance to see how they took the journey. Major Henry Shucksmith, a Leeds surgeon, and his Field Surgical Unit also pulled out in the morning — leaving us on our own. He would not travel in a three-tonner and borrowed a Jeep for the journey.

Tuesday April 18th 1944

I slept very well last night, there was very little noise. But have decided to move my bivvy nearer the theatre and so commenced to dig out a new site.

At night when I got into my sleeping bag, I felt something moving near my feet. It was a rat, but quite friendly and appeared upset when I turned the bag inside out.

Wednesday April 19th

Three shells landed uncomfortably close while I was operating on an abdominal case. A stone rolled down the hill and went through the roof of the quarter-master's truck.

Sunday April 23rd

Operating all last night. Jerry set fire to some of our vehicles in the wadi and shelled them continuously. Planes came over and machine gunned near us in the afternoon. Casualties arrived from shelling both up and down the wadi.

I moved my bivvy to a hopefully safer spot.

Monday April 24th

A very busy and noisy day from our shelling and from the Bosch.

The Assistant Director of Medical Service 78th Div., Col. Gilroy, came to see us. His H.Q. had been divebombed in the afternoon.

Tuesday April 25th

Not feeling too well, developed diarrhoea and vomiting. The Poles arrived before mid-day and commenced to take over. Alan Hollinrake, my anaesthetist, went to bed with a temperature of 101 degrees. My men are tired and not well.

Thursday April 27th

We spent the whole of yesterday evacuating casualties and packing our equipment. Alan Hollinrake, who is not well, accompanied them to a base hospital.

This afternoon I left with the remainder of my unit. I drove the Jeep and chose the 'Inferno' track via Verafro, stopping for the night near to an Indian Casualty Clearing Station.

The Polish surgical team who took over from Geoffrey Wooler in Inferno Valley, and who were all killed by German artillery two days later.

Friday April 28th 1944

Visited 13 Corps and obtained four days' leave. Checked over our equipment in the afternoon.

Sunday April 30th

Last night the Germans moved their heavy artillery guns on alignment with the 'Inferno Valley', lining directly up it. They killed the Polish surgeon who had taken over from me and many of his personnel. His theatre was completely wrecked. The Poles had fixed their operating tent on exactly the same position where mine had been, and I had assured them that I thought it was the safest place in the wadi.

The Germans do not respect the Polish red cross because they say that the Poles are using it for storing ammunition, and they also carry ammunition in their ambulances. I do not think this is true.

Tuesday May 2nd

We were given four days' leave, which we spent at Positano on the Sorrento peninsular. After a restful four days we drove to Pompei and lunched at the 70th General Hospital.

Major Barbara Stimson (daughter of the American Secretary for War) is working at the hospital in charge of an orthopaedic unit.

After lunch we drove to Vairano, about three miles South of Cassino, to join the 2nd Indian Casualty Clearing Station.

Thursday 11th May 1944

Great preparations for a colossal push in the Cassino area. Everybody full of confidence and saying we are heading for Rome.

An Indian division and the British 4th division go into action at 11 pm tonight. We commence duty rosta of sixteen hours on and eight hours off at midnight. Our theatre is well prepared for anything.

Friday May 12th to Tuesday May 16th

Very busy operating day and night, did about forty cases of which six were abdominal injuries. I was very tired towards the end.

Wednesday May 17th

Brigadier Stammers came to see us. All the abdominal cases are still alive, which rather surprised him, but he only arrived just in time because one died in the afternoon, after he had left.

Thursday May 18th

Had the whole day off, so took the unit through Piedmonte d'Alife up to Lago Matese, where we had lunch. We could not quite reach there in the 15-cwt because of a blown bridge so had to walk the last half mile. News that we are moving immediately to a Field Dressing Station. We shall miss the Indians. They are pleasant people to work with. Their food is better than ours, and I had two orderlies looking after me instead of one part-time batman.

Their doctors were responsible for resuscitating casualties when they arrived, and also looked after the cases post-operatively, when I had finished with them in the theatre.

One day I asked the doctor in charge of the post-operative ward to give a patient one pint of plasma intravenously. Between cases I went into the ward to see how this patient was progressing.

Plasma is a slightly yellow opaque liquid, but the fluid this patient was receiving was a darker yellow and clear. I was puzzled, because it also had a froth on it. I disconnected the bottle, the contents smelt of aniseed. He was in fact receiving a cough mixture intravenously, and did not even cough. I changed it to plasma and he recovered.

Saturday May 20th 1944

Cassino and the monastery fell two days ago. Our tanks are past Aquino, we shall be moving soon.

Sunday May 21st

Brig. Cheyne called in last night to tell us that we are going forward in two days. The advance is proceeding rapidly. Casualties started to arrive in the morning and we were extremely busy operating all day until after midnight. Then we received orders to move forward immediately. The men were packing until 2 am.

Monday May 22nd

We left the site near S. Vittore about noon and moved up Route 6 through Cassino to a position West of the town and on the North bank of the Rapido river. Cassino is not recognisable as a town and all the rock face leading up to the monastery is peppered with shell bursts. The outer walls of the monastery are still standing.

We set up with 2 Field Dressing Station next to 11 Main Dressing Station on the Gustav line. Never have I seen such elaborate dugouts as those made by the Germans. Many have doors and are panelled with wood inside. We pitched our tent next to a former German slit trench, because we are still within shell range and three days ago the site was bombed and strafed from the air.

Many dead are still lying about in the fields: a party of South Africans are very busy burying them, which took them ten days. The smell is terrible.

The ground is so rough and full of so many trenches that we had to bulldoze the site before we could pitch the tents.

I was most surprised to see fireflies (flying glow worms) at night, dozens of them glowing intermittently and flying between the remains of trees.

Gordon with 23 Field Surgical Unit is also here at the Field Dressing Station.

Tuesday May 23rd

A heavy artillery baggage commenced at dawn. News came through later in the morning that the Poles have taken Mt. Cairo and are now fighting for Piedemonte.

Brig. Stammers came to see us and told us only to operate on the very bad cases.

The surgical team examining dug-outs at Cassino. In the photograph above, they are gathered round a wooden cross with a German name on it.

After the bombardment — trees near the Rapido river near Monte Cassino.

Wednesday May 24th 1944

Busy most of the day operating and reorganising equipment.
There was an air raid last night and had to take cover in a trench.

Saturday May 27th

We stayed overnight at our position near San Angelo on the Gustav line to look after a severely injured Canadian and to hand him over to Field Dressing Station when it arrived.

Then after breakfast we left, I drove the Dodge and followed Ace track which is a new road we have made parallel to Route 6 through fields full of shell holes and bomb craters to Aquino which is absolutely in ruins. There we turned right on to Route 6 and followed the main road to Rome for another two miles, where opposite Castrocielo we joined 152 Main Dressing Station with 78 Div.

Sunday May 28th

The noisiest night I have ever experienced. There was gunfire the whole time without respite. At midnight a colossal barrage opened up, every type of

Aftermath of battle. Scenes reminiscent of the First World War in Aquino, a village beyond Cassino.

gun seemed to be firing, all of them were behind us and some of the 25-pounders in the same field.

Yesterday the small strategic town of Arce was taken by the Allies but Jerry counter-attacked at dawn and retook the place. Then at about 8 am our artillery opened up again and we watched Arce being pounded, for it was less than four miles away.

A German observation post on a hill about two miles away received a battering. The Irish guards were sent in and retook the town. Jerry threw over a few shells in the morning aiming at the crossroads on Route 6. I saw one burst about four hundred yards away. In the afternoon he sent a lot over our heads towards the bridge over the Melfa river but did not hit it.

In the afternoon the C.O's batman gave a short service because we could not obtain a padre.

Monday May 29th

Col. Lytle returned at midday and told us to proceed at once to Ceprano with their ambulance cars. We followed the road by the side of the Melfa river and then across country along a newly constructed track until we joined the Ceprano-Gaeta road.

In Ceprano there were four dead Germans on the ground floor of the house where we had been ordered to open our theatre, and they smelt badly. I disliked the sickly smell, we had had more than enough in Cassino, so I found another house with a country smell because the Germans had kept horses in it. I preferred a farm smell to that of decaying humans. We opened up the theatre in this second house. I operated all night and until 3.00 pm the following day.

Tuesday May 30th

Jerry shells landed fairly near during the night but they caused no casualties.

Stammers came to see us in the afternoon and hoped to send another Field Surgical Unit tomorrow.

My batman washed all my clothes, so when I got up in the late afternoon I put them on after having a bath and then went out into the garden: just as the Germans started shelling again and one fell in the garden not far away from me. I fell down on my face under a tree, but unfortunately the Germans had been there before me using it as a toilet. My clothes were filthy again and I heard my batman, who came from Manchester, say: 'Hey look at 'im mucked up again'.

Thursday June 1st

An engineer informed us that the bodies in the first house, where we had been told to set up our operating theatre, were mined. Wires around the bodies were attached to mines in the cellar. So it is as well that we did not move them, otherwise we should not be here. We have more respect for our dead than the Germans. Using them as booby traps is unthinkable.

8
Rome Liberated

Tuesday June 6th 1944

The invasion of France commenced. We and 'A' Field Dressing Station left Frosinore after breakfast. I went a devious route through Alatri, Fiuggi to Acuto where we stopped for a cup of tea at 'C' Field Dressing Station. They are in a fine building which is untouched.

Then we went on through Gerazzano to Palestrina. There was one continuous stream of traffic along this road and it was almost static. We saw many burnt out German tanks and vehicles.

We joined Route 6 at Valmontone, which has been flattened, then went along towards Rome. We could just see the dome of St. Peter's in the distance

Geoffrey Wooler's surgical team en route to Rome.

before we started dropping down on to the plain where we are to pitch our tents.

Wednesday June 7th 1944

The fighting is now around Tivoli where the 6th Armoured Division with the 4th Infantry Division are attacking. Col. Watson, the consulting orthopaedic surgeon, arrived before lunch.

Thursday June 8th

Col. Watson took Harmer and myself into Rome and we spent the whole day looking round the place even though it was out of bounds. Unfortunately it was a festive day and all the shops were shut.

We sat down under some palm trees in the Piazza Venezia and cooked sausages and brewed tea, much to the amusement of the Italians, seeing a British Colonel and two Majors cooking.

Thursday June 15th

Got up at 5.00 am and packed the lorries. Left Vallerano about 8.00 am.

Found 166 Light Field Ambulance near Orvieto which had only been cleared of Bosch this morning. Col. Keeling is now their Commanding Officer. It was a glorious day so I wandered out into some nearby fields to see and collect some wild flowers. I was photographing some particularly attractive flowers when a head popped up out of the grass. I said: 'Deutsch nicht wahr? Sie müssen mit mir kommen'. (German are you not? You must come with me.) I had no revolver on me and he offered no resistance. I gave him a cigarette and he showed me where a vehicle was buried in a nearby farm under a load of hay. It was a small Opel truck riddled with shell holes, but I was able to drive it. My prisoner was a cook, and he was the only prisoner I ever succeeded in taking.

Saturday June 17th

We have been ordered to go to Castiglione del Lago — which is on Lake Trasamene.

Sunday June 18th

The dressing station closed and moved off in the morning. We packed and left in the afternoon. Proceeding along the road to Castiglione we were concerned that the traffic became less and less. We stopped at a roadside farm where the farmer appeared to be just leaving with all his belongings, he assured

Above: Col Watson and Major Harmer cooking sausages and brewing tea in the Piazza Venezia, near Trajan's Column, Rome. Italians looked on with amused incredulity. Below: Geoffrey Wooler in the Piazza Venezia two days after the liberation of Rome.

us that we were on the correct road, so on we continued with the three-tonners until we saw some of our men in a ditch at the side of the road. We asked them if it was the correct road, they said it was, but Castiglione was still in Bosch hands and they were the front line. We turned the three-tonners around as quickly as possible and retreated as fast as we could; only to find that the farm where we had first made enquiries had been demolished by shell fire. Major Jagger, the Deputy Director of Medical Services (DDMS), met us on the return journey. He told me to get into his Jeep and took me up a mountain to the Advanced Dressing Station of 20th Field Ambulance (South African) where I operated throughout the night on cases they could not evacuate.

Next morning I returned to my unit with a barrel of South African brandy.

Friday July 14th 1944

I stayed the night at the Buffani Palace Hotel in Perugia which is a leave hotel for officers. In the morning explored Assisi, then went to Deruta where I bought two coffee services, some plates and a decorative plant pot (which I still have today).

Saturday July 15th

Paid another visit to the monastery at Assisi then packed all my crockery. Left Assisi about 11.00 am and drove the Dodge straight to Rome, arriving about 4.00 pm.

Sunday July 16th

All officers serving with the Royal Army Medical Corps were invited to an audience with the Pope at 10.00 am in the Vatican.

We arrived about ten minutes earlier, and were escorted by the Swiss Guards up the long staircase from St. Peter's Square into a large chamber on

An audience with the Pope.

the first floor of the Vatican. Altogether there were about seventy of us. We arranged ourselves in a single line around the periphery of the chamber.

Promptly at 10.00 am the Pope entered walking and escorted by two cardinals. He spoke in English to each officer in turn asking about their experiences in the war and about the conditions in England, etc.

Major Barbara Stimson was the only lady in the room. She wore a British battledress with a khaki skirt to match. She had the crowns on her shoulders showing that she was a major. Her hair was cut short almost like a man's — a sort of Eton crop — and she had her campaign medals on her large chest. The Pope looked puzzled when he confronted her, and more puzzled still when she spoke with a female voice. I was informed later that the Pope should never look down when talking to someone, but on this occasion he broke the rule and looked down. He saw she was wearing a skirt. He smiled and was obviously greatly relieved.

After being given a small emblem of St. Peter we received the Papal blessing and then departed. I lunched at a restaurant in the Pincio gardens overlooking the city of Rome.

Monday July 17th 1944

Spent the whole morning looking around St. Peter's. Climbed up to the ball under the cross on top of the dome. In the afternoon swam in the Tiber and found I was not strong enough to swim against the current.

Thursday July 20th

Left Rome after breakfast driving the German Blitz Opel. It had no windscreen and the body was riddled with shell holes. A main bearing was making a noise, and I was afraid that the engine might break down any time. Alan sat at the front with me and we were all so happy that we were going on a week's leave to Sorrento. We sang most of the way. The road was crowded with Italians returning South with as much as they could carry. We gave lifts to as many people as our vehicles would hold. Near Frascati there were eight nuns signalling for a lift. We managed to help them on to the back of the Opel and then carried on South. After several miles, when the nuns discovered that we were making for Naples, they were not pleased and wanted me to take them to Isernia nearer to the East coast. I suggested that they should obtain another lift — but they refused to leave.

We stopped for lunch by the side of the Rapido at Cassino to see some familiar ground.

I suggested to the nuns again that they should find another vehicle going

East, because we wanted to reach Naples as soon as possible, but they did not move off the back of the Opel.

My boys had an idea, it was a hot day, so after lunch a few of them took off all their clothes and dived into the Rapido naked. The nuns fled.

Monday July 24th 1944

Staying at the 70th General in Pompei I shared a room with Rodney Smith (now Lord Rodney Smith). He had received a leg injury at the Anzio landings which had damaged the external peroneal nerve. Tomorrow he was leaving for England, and consented to take all my crockery from Deruta with him.

Tuesday July 25th

I drove Rodney to the docks at Naples in my 15 cwt. truck. A party of American soldiers were loading the hospital ship *Oranje*. I asked their officer if he would load my two boxes of crockery from Deruta. He gladly consented, and offered to load my truck as well.

On arriving in England, Rodney would dispatch them to my home, and I was glad to be relieved of them.

Friday July 28th

We were on four days' leave in Positano, when we received orders to join 13th Corps just South of Florence. Our leave finished, we had a short time in Rome and then proceeded North towards Florence.

Wednesday Aug. 9th

We were billeted on the South bank of the Arno, in the Castle Uzzano belonging to a Count Castelbarco-Albani.

The Count arrived from Rome this morning with a young Italian partisan officer. Both spoke good French and I had a long conversation with them. His wife is in his apartment in Florence, which is situated on the North side of the Arno adjoining the San Trinita bridge. He knew the bridge had been destroyed, but he wondered whether his property had been damaged. I took him to the South side of the Arno in my Jeep, he looked at his apartment through field glasses and was relieved to see it had not been damaged, but he did not see his wife.

Thursday Aug. 10th

I was asked by Major Jagger (DDMS) if I would volunteer to inspect the condition of the hospitals in Florence. An American colonel took me in his

Jeep as far as the outskirts of the town where we were met by an English boy who lives in Florence: and he acted as my guide.

While in the garden of American Medical Group Headquarters a shell fell not very far away causing a number of civilian casualties. We went to the civilian hospital to see how they would be treated. There I met Professor Pietro Valdoni, who was working in great difficulty, having no water — so the instruments were being sort of sterilised in alcohol. He was performing all operations with only local anaesthesia. He asked me if I would take a young Italian doctor back with me and teach him how to administer a general anaesthetic, to which I gladly consented.

There was a great deal of machine gun and rifle fire going on in the streets and we had to walk a mile through houses, gardens and olive groves in order to reach the military hospital — we were told that we were the first allied officers to go there. Had a glass of wine with the Colonel in charge, then returned to the Jeep. Called on an American woman whose child was ill.

Friday Aug. 11th 1944

We left the Castle Uzzano and went to another large house nearer to Florence. It belongs to an Austrian Jew. We are attached to No. 54 Field Dressing Station and we are all under canvas in the gardens of the house.

Wednesday Aug. 16th

Brig. Cheyne took me into Florence to see a Canadian who had been wounded and was being treated in an Italian hospital. We crossed the Arno over a Bailey bridge which had only been finished this morning, and came back over the Ponte Vecchio.

The Bosch were dropping a few shells but the city is much quieter now and I heard no small arms fire this time.

Friday Aug. 18th

My anaesthetist — Alan Hollinrake — has been teaching the young Italian for eight days. We thought he was sufficiently competent to give a general anaesthetic himself so I took him back to the civilian hospital in Florence to see how he would perform.

Professor Pietro Valdoni's first case was a cholecystectomy on a very large woman who was strapped down firmly to the operating table. There was a considerable number of young doctors in the theatre, so that I had not a good view of the operation. The first thing that alerted me was the patient screaming 'Oh, mamma mia!'

The young Italian, being rather nervous of using ether for the first time, had not even put the patient to sleep before Pietro started to make an incision. He turned to me saying 'Anaesthetic no good' which was all the English he knew at this time.

I tried in French, saying 'Mais elle n'est pas si profonde', which everyone quite rightly did not understand. So, I followed it with 'Les yeux ne sont pas si grands'.

The lighting in the theatre was poor, so an Italian doctor lit his cigarette lighter to examine the patient's eyes: the resulting ether explosion took away her eyebrows and part of her hair.

Saturday Aug. 19th 1944

The following day, I volunteered to start the anaesthetic, which I did as neatly as a surgeon could, with a mixture of alcohol, chloroform and ether and then changed to pure ether. Pietro made an incision without any problem, and so I handed over the responsibility of the anaesthesia to the young Italian.

He was in a liberal mood to-day and a fair quantity of ether spilled on to the floor.

It was cold inside the theatre for August. The operating theatre was an unusual shape, rather like a corridor with the table at one end. Pietro in Italian asked a theatre attendant to switch on an old electric fire, which was at the far end of the theatre. It took about 10 minutes for the ether to reach it and then there was a really big explosion which swept through the whole theatre. Everybody fled, convinced that the building had been bombed, and I was the only one left with the patient.

Fortunately, both patients survived, being somewhat disfigured, perhaps the families were told that it was due to enemy action. But — two ether explosions in two days is not bad.

Wednesday Aug. 23rd

We received orders to move towards the Adriatic coast of Italy where the Germans have created the so-called Gothic Line.

Monday Sept. 18th

We have been extremely busy during the past ten days and so have had no time to write my diary. We are all very tired. The advance towards Rimini has been costly for 5 Corps have had five thousand casualties.

Brigadier Stammers came to see me and told me that our cases were doing well at the base hospital. He was obviously pleased and asked me to operate on the next one hundred cases performing a primary suture.

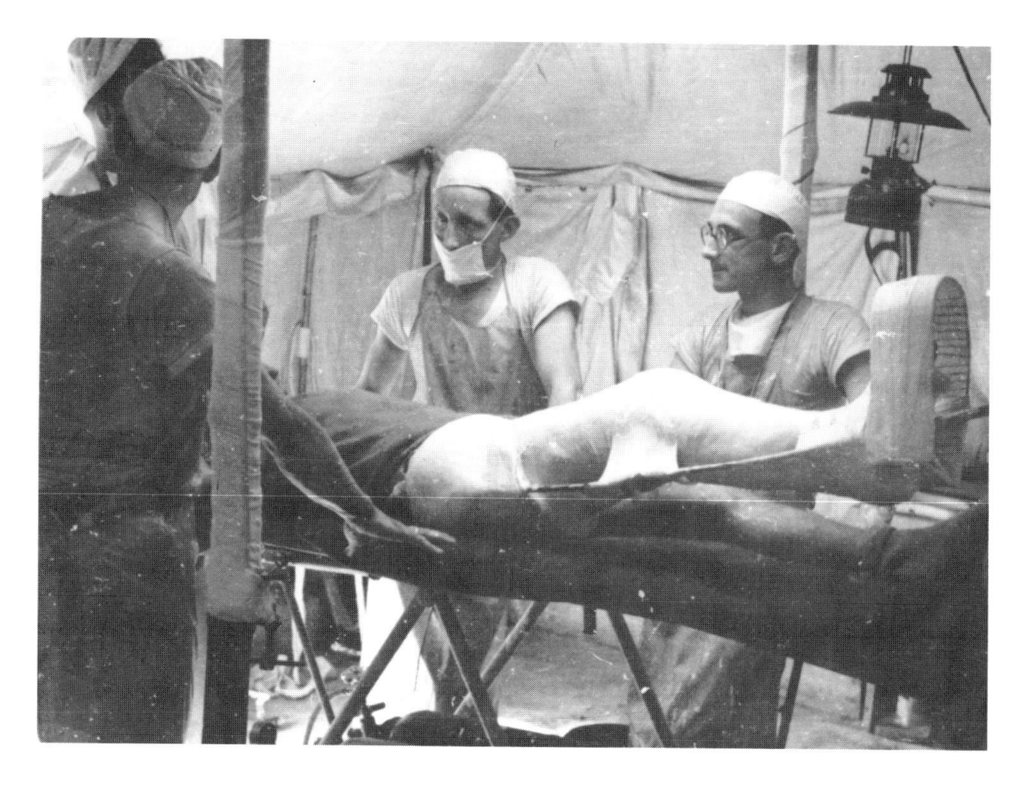

A front-line operating theatre lit by a Tilley lamp.

This evening the first case to arrive was a Lieut. Nahum Baron. He had a large shell wound of the left shoulder which I excised and then performed a primary suture and because this was the first case on which I had carried out this technique I photographed his injury. After the war he became photographer to the Royal Family and mentioned me in his autobiography.

Wednesday Oct. 4th 1944

We are in Cattolica with the 5th Canadian Casualty Clearing Station. The Canadian sisters had asked their forward troops to bring back a captured vehicle for them.

I had acquired a Jeep and the German Opel when we were in Orvieto. I did not wish to part with either of them, even though I had as well my normal complement of two 3-tonners and one 15 cwt. The sisters were living in a large house near the hospital and there was also a large garden at the rear.

Because there was insufficient water to flush the toilets, the Canadian pioneer corps dug latrines for them in the back garden. Now Canadians do not dig latrines like our men do — they are what you might term 'short and shallow' ones so they last for only a few days and the site has to be continually changed.

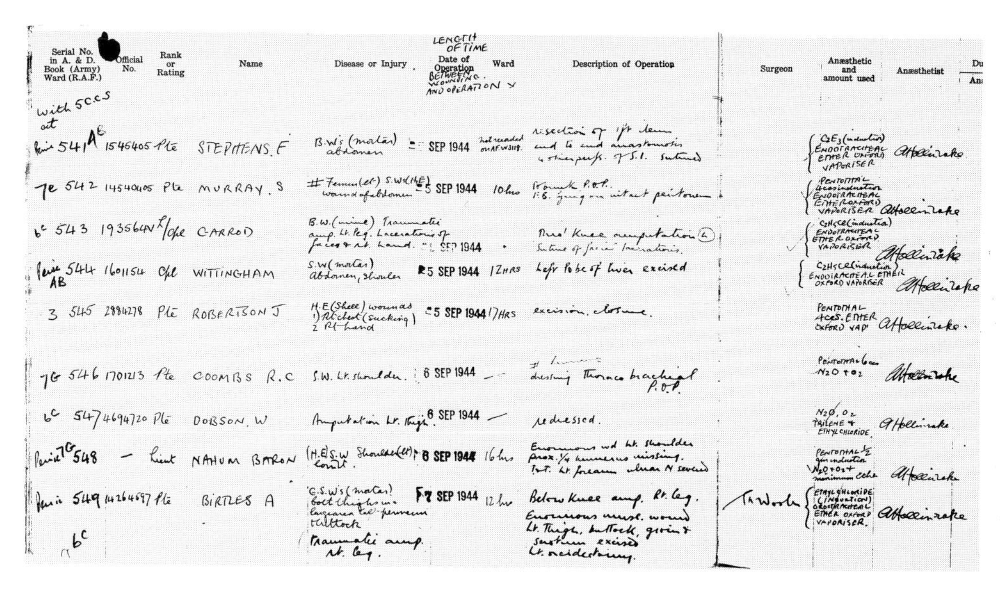

with 5 C.C.S. at

Serial No. in A. & D. Book (Army) Ward (R.A.F.)	Official No.	Rank or Rating	Name	Disease or Injury	Date of Operation (Length of time between wounding and operation)	Ward	Description of Operation	Surgeon	Anæsthetic and amount used	Anæsthetist
541 AB	1546405	Pte	STEPHENS. F	B.W's (mortar) abdomen	SEP 1944	not recorded on AF W3118	Resection of [illegible] end to end anastomosis [illegible] sutured		C_2E_3 (induction) Endotracheal Ether Oxford Vaporiser	A Hollinrake
542	14540405	Pte	MURRAY. S	# Femur (Lt) S.Ws (H.E) wound of abdomen	5 SEP 1944	10 hrs	[illegible] P.O.P. [illegible] intact peritoneum		Pentothal [illegible] induction Endotracheal Ether (Oxford) Vaporiser	A Hollinrake
543	1935644	L/Cpl	CARROD	B.W. (mine) Traumatic amp. Lt. leg. Lacerations of face & rt. hand.	SEP 1944		Thro' knee amputation. Suture of facial lacerations.		C_2H_5Cl (induction) Endotracheal Ether Oxford Vaporiser	A Hollinrake
544 AB	1601154	Cpl	WITTINGHAM	S.W (mortar) abdomen, shoulder	5 SEP 1944	12 HRS	Left lobe of liver excised		C_2H_5Cl (induction) Endotracheal Ether Oxford Vaporiser	A Hollinrake
3 545	2884278	Pte	ROBERTSON J	H.E (Shell) wounds 1) Rt chest (sucking) 2 Rt hand	5 SEP 1944	17 HRS	excision. closure.		Pentothal 4ccs. Ether Oxford Vap	A Hollinrake.
7G 546	1701213	Pte	COOMBS R.C	S.W. Lt. shoulder.	6 SEP 1944	—	dressing Thoraco brachial P.O.P.		Pentothal 6ccs $N_2O + O_2$	A Hollinrake
6C 547	4694720	Pte	DOBSON, W	Amputation Lt. thigh.	6 SEP 1944	—	redressed.		N_2O, O_2 Trilene + Ethyl chloride.	A Hollinrake
7G 548	—	Lieut	NAHUM BARON	(H.E) S.W Shoulder (Lt) [illegible]	6 SEP 1944	16 hrs	Enormous wd Lt. shoulder prox. 1/4 humerus missing. [illegible] Lt. forearm ulnar N severed		Pentothal 1/2 gm induction $N_2O + O_2$ + minimum ether	A Hollinrake
549 6C	14264597	Pte	BIRTLES A	G.S.W's (mortar) both thighs [illegible] [illegible] perineum buttock. Traumatic amp. rt. leg.	7 SEP 1944	12 hrs	Below knee amp. Rt. leg. Enormous musc. wound Lt. thigh, buttock, groin & scrotum excised Lt. orchidectomy.	[illegible] Wooler	Ethyl chloride (induction) Endotracheal Ether Oxford Vaporiser.	A Hollinrake

Above: an extract from Geoffrey Wooler's operating book including the name of Lieut Nahum Baron. Right: an honourable mention in Baron's autobiography

‘I found myself in bed, absorbing blood transfusion after blood transfusion until I could take no more. Every hour fresh loads of wounded piled in to make the discomfort and the stench worse. We had taken a bad beating on San Coriano Ridge, and had suffered many thousands of casualties to no purpose. What went wrong I still do not know. Then I did not care. All I could think of was my own wound. By some miracle a soldier passing my bed dropped my camera by my side. It was unharmed, and I took that as a good omen. The doctors had more to do than they could cope with.

One, Major Wooler, a boy still in his twenties, with a face like a nun, was moving cheerfully from bed to bed when I beckoned to him. "Major," I said, "I can't take any more blood transfusions. Can't you operate on me?

He did not reply to that. "What were you doing to get a packet like that?" he asked. I told him about the white pigeon, and he laughed. "What a way to die," he said amiably. "I'm an amateur photographer myself, you know. I'll take a picture of this wound and send it to you in England. Yes," he added, changing the subject abruptly, "I'll operate on you."

"And, Doctor," I said, "don't take my arm off if you can help it. That's a special request."

"Don't worry," he said. "I won't." Wooler was as good as his word. He did send me a photograph of my wound, but I have lost it. If he reads these words I hope he will come to my studio and have his picture taken free. I know now, although I did not then, that he saved my life.’

A photograph Geoffrey Wooler 'liberated' from Rocca della Caminate, Mussolini's refuge in the mountains near Forli. He is seen second right with one of his generals.

The fourth site had been chosen, and the Canadians started to dig before lunch. But this new site alerted the whole local Italian community. When the Canadians stopped work for lunch an army of Italians arrived with shovels, for hidden under this fourth site there was a Fiat saloon car. The hole in which it had been kept was lined with wood and when the car was brought out it was in excellent condition. After lunch practically all personnel from the Casualty Clearing Station arrived to watch and I heard one Canadian sister say: 'Well I am damned and there was one in our backyard'.

Friday Oct. 20th 1944

I spent the day in bed then operated again throughout the night. We have had an extremely busy time dealing with the most severe injuries for the past two months with no respite.

My anaesthetist became very depressed, saying that he had had enough. He walked out of the theatre last night refusing to anaesthetise any more cases. I was fortunate because one of the Canadian Medical Officers came to help me and proved to be a good anaesthetist.

Serial No. in A. & D. Book (Army) Ward (R.A.F.)	Official No.	Rank or Rating	Name	Disease or Injury	Date of Operation	Ward	Description of Operation
1008	—	—		S.W. Lt. chest wall & Rt. forehead.	22/11/44.		excision
1009	5574372	Pte.	SPAULDING M.V.	B.W. (aerial) comp. Lt. fib involving ankle joint.	22/11/44.		excision bilat. P.of.
1010	4806833	Pte.	CROOK R.	S.W. (H.E.) Left buttock & right cheek.	22/11/44.		excision.
1011	14604709	Pte.	DEAN P.	S.W. (H.E.) Comp. left scap. Sucking wd lt. chest.	22/11/44.		excision, intercostals ligated. Laparotomy.
1012	14269684	Pte.	RICKLER G E	S.W. left knee	22/11/44.		Amputation lower 1/3 thigh.
1013	14579347	Pte.	RUTTLEDGE	S.W. (H.E.) abdominal wall.	22/11/44.		excision.
1014	6846778	Rfn.	ENGLISH. A 1st. KRRC	B.W. (Mine) Bilat. comp. tarsus, left tibia & rt. femur	23/11/44.		Bilateral lower 1/3 thigh amputations.
1015	P.o.w.	Gft.	KNOBEL.	a) [illegible] b) Penetrating wound abdo. wall. Prolapse of small of small intestine.	23.11.44.		[illegible]
1016	871030	L/Cpl.	TUCK G.L.	S.W. [illegible] T&T lt. chest (posterior).	24.11.44		intercostal vessels ligated muscles layers closed.
1017. (10)	6848869	Sgt.	KING. G 1st. KRRC	B.W. (mortar) Lt. arm.			excision F.B. removed.

An extract from Geoffrey Wooler's operating book from November 1994.

Friday Nov. 24th 1944

Spent the morning in bed. Then received orders from 5 Corps to move at once to 57 Field Dressing Station in Forli. So packed and left Cesana after lunch bringing our goose George with us. Arrived in Forli as it was becoming dark — a lot of traffic on the road. My boys set up the theatre and I went to bed early. Wheeler with his Field Surgical Unit is also at 57 Field Dressing Station and he offered to stand in for us tonight because we are all very tired. The third night we were there our goose George disappeared and we were convinced that he had been stolen. Now this bird had got to know us amazingly well, he answered to a particular whistle and his name.

Our dental officer went around the buildings in Forli whistling and calling 'George'. He answered from a basement house where some of our troops were billeted. They denied that they had him: so our dental officer again whistled, George answered and was returned to his friends.

I was glad I was away from my unit at Christmas, because he was served for dinner. I would have walked out.

9
The End of the War

There was a surgical congress in Rome from February 12th to 17th 1945. As many as possible of British and American medical personnel serving in the Mediterranean area attended — altogether about three hundred. I spoke about the initial surgery of limb injuries and mentioned that in the desert the 8th Army had not found it necessary to perform as wide an incision as we had been accustomed to do in the 1st Army because the desert sand is relatively sterile.

The congress was a great success from both scientific and social points of view. It was a chance to meet old friends, and relate experiences of being five years at war.

I was very glad to meet Barbara Stimson again. I had met her first in Oxford at the new Churchill Hospital where she quickly gained an enormous reputation, for she brought with her from the States the method of nailing or plating together fractured bones, which allowed the patient to get out of bed the day after the operation and be discharged in about two weeks. This was of tremendous advantage to a patient with a fractured femur who might otherwise be kept in bed for three months with his leg on traction and then in plaster.

Barbara was of inestimable value to us during the war — even compound fractures healed quickly using her method and penicillin.

We dined together at the Officers' Club in the Pincio gardens one evening. The following day the Pope invited all delegates attending the conference to meet him in the Vatican. It would be my second audience with the Pope but this was of a more formal character presumably because well over three hundred people attended. He was carried down the centre of the room seated on a chair. He had little chance of speaking to everybody, but he did stop and speak to a few as he was carried across the room and back, he blessed everybody as he went. It was not quite the same as my previous encounter, when there were few of us and he spoke to everyone present in turn.

Immediately after the meeting I returned to my unit in North Italy. We continued to be extremely busy and in twelve weeks dealt with over five hundred

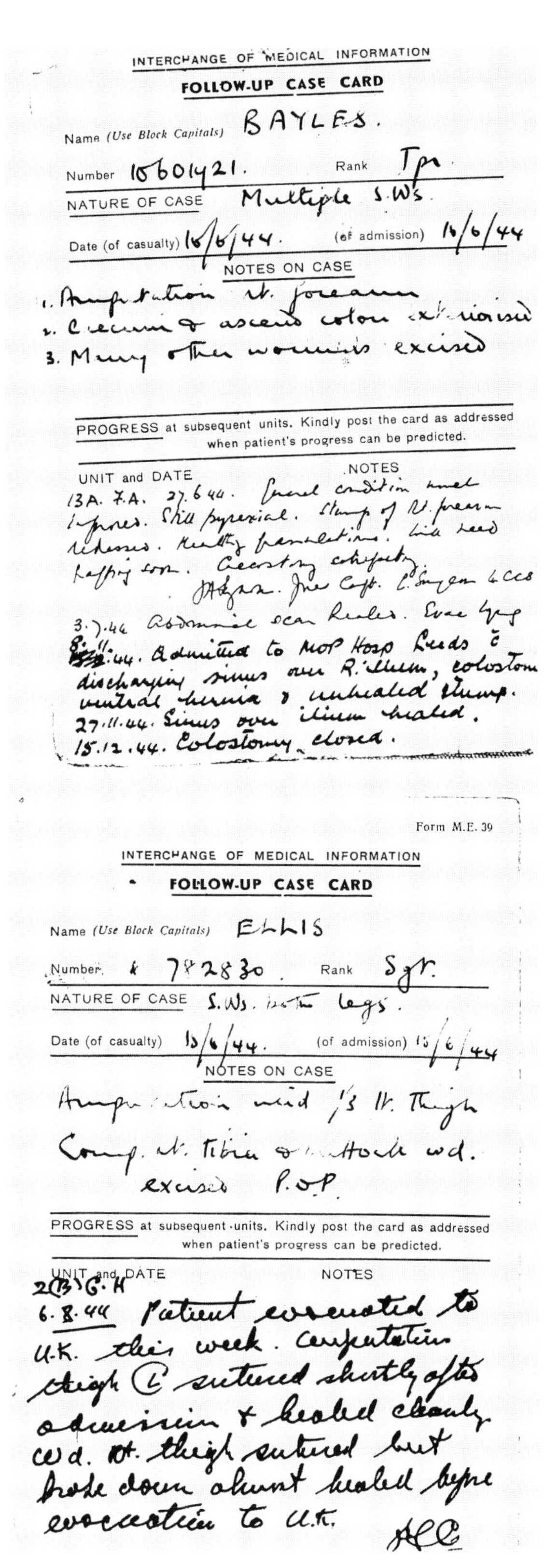

INTERCHANGE OF MEDICAL INFORMATION

FOLLOW-UP CASE CARD

Name (Use Block Capitals) BAYLES.

Number 1560421. Rank Tpr.

NATURE OF CASE Multiple S.W's.

Date (of casualty) 16/6/44. (of admission) 16/6/44

NOTES ON CASE

1. Amputation rt. forearm
2. Caecum & ascend colon exteriorised
3. Many other wounds excised

PROGRESS at subsequent units. Kindly post the card as addressed when patient's progress can be predicted.

UNIT and DATE NOTES

13A. 7.A. 27.6.44. General condition much improved. Still pyrexial. Stump of R. forearm [illegible]. [illegible] [illegible] [illegible] Colostomy [illegible]. [illegible] Capt. [illegible] Surgeon [illegible]

3.7.44 Abdominal scar healed. Evac [illegible]

[illegible].11.44. Admitted to MOP Hosp Leeds c discharging sinus over R. ileum, colostomy ventral hernia & unhealed stump.

27.11.44. Sinus over ilium healed.

15.12.44. Colostomy closed.

Form M.E. 39

INTERCHANGE OF MEDICAL INFORMATION

FOLLOW-UP CASE CARD

Name (Use Block Capitals) ELLIS

Number 4 782830. Rank Sgt.

NATURE OF CASE S.Ws. both legs.

Date (of casualty) 13/6/44. (of admission) 13/6/44

NOTES ON CASE

Amputation mid 1/3 lt. thigh

Comp. rt. tibia & [illegible] wd. excised P.O.P.

PROGRESS at subsequent units. Kindly post the card as addressed when patient's progress can be predicted.

UNIT and DATE NOTES

2(B) G.H 6.8.44 Patient evacuated to U.K. this week. Amputation thigh (L) sutured shortly after admission & healed cleanly. Wd. Rt. thigh sutured but broke down almost healed before evacuation to U.K. [illegible]

priority one cases. My boys were getting tired, they had worked now for three years in a Field Surgical Unit. They were the same team that I had taken over from John Latchmore who had trained them when they landed in North Africa in December, 1942.

Also I was getting worried that I might lose my second anaesthetist when one morning Brigadier Harold Edwards came to see us.

He thought that we had earned a rest, and as the war in Italy was drawing to a close he sent us back to work with D'Abreu at the 98th General Hospital in Bari.

The 98th General was in a new hospital built by Mussolini. It became a sort of collecting place for many of the forward units, now that the war had almost finished. There was really little for us to do, and I spent most of the time swimming in the Adriatic. The officers had commandeered a house in Trani which was on the beach, an attractive place steeped in history for it was from here that

Examples of surgical cards showing the nature of injuries and their treatment.

the Crusaders set out in the 11th and 12th centuries to try and win back the Holy Land.

On May 1st the Germans surrendered on the Italian front, and on May 7th they accepted unconditional surrender. I continued to be surgeon on duty, rotating with the other surgeons, but there was little to do.

One day when I was on duty, a soldier from Yugoslavia was admitted with an entry wound in his left chest, and when I operated on him I found that the bullet was embedded in the wall of the descending aorta. After it was removed the aorta did not bleed but bulged a little, so I reinforced it with a patch. About a week later I took this soldier in my car with a number of others to see something different from a hospital ward. I went for a swim in the sea and was horrified to see the Yugoslav dive in later after me — fortunately the patch held. Early movement is good for you — but this was a bit too early.

Another time when I was on duty a well dressed Italian came to see me and called himself Professor Cecorelli. He practised psychiatry and hypnosis in Bari, and speaking good English he told me that one surgeon in Bari preferred to operate on his patients while hypnotised rather than under a general anaesthetic — which I can well believe because they are not able to give a good general anaesthetic, as I learnt in Florence.

He offered his services free, and thinking it would be interesting I suggested that he came back tomorrow, after I had spoken to the commanding officer and obtained volunteers from the men. The commanding officer was agreeable, and I obtained two volunteers, one had a subacute appendicitis and the other an inguinal hernia.

The professor returned next morning, my anaesthetist and I waited in the theatre to see if hypnosis could be successful. The professor took the first patient into an adjoining room, and soon he was wheeled into the operating theatre, unconscious but his abdomen was as hard as a drum, all his muscles contracted. They did not relax by repeated commands from the professor, so not to waste more time, my anaesthetist put him to sleep, and I removed his appendix.

The next patient was taken into the side room by the professor and after about ten minutes started to howl, then there was a loud scream and he rushed through the operating theatre out into a corridor with practically no clothing on — for he was the hernia case.

The professor apologised and said that the whole atmosphere was not correct, the hospital was too noisy etc. I thanked him, and deterred him from returning the following day.

The European war being over, the number of surgical admissions rapidly diminished. I decided to go to Venice. I spent four days on leave there, it was my first visit and I enjoyed it immensely. There were also many of my friends staying at the same leave hotel. We had many happy moments discussing our experiences. On June 4th I flew back to Bari.

GONDOLA TARIFF

Don't pay more!

Be firm, these are the rates!

Tariff for all MILITARY PERSONNEL in uniform is set out hereunder :

(a) Gondolas-Service with one gondolier

		0600 to 2200	2200 to 0600
1	Hire of gondola for one half-hour or fraction thereof, for 3 persons	20	30
2.	Each additional half-hour or fraction	15	30
3	Each additional person over 3	5	8

For this service with 2 gondoliers, the tariff is doubled,

(b) ALL CRAFT OTHER THAN GONDOLAS: Service with 1 Oarsman.

		0600 to 2200	2200 to 0600
1	Hire of craft for one half-hour or fraction thereof, for 3 persons	14	20
2.	Each additional half-hour or fraction	10	20
3.	Each additional person over 3	4	6

For this service with 2 oarsmen the tariff is doubled.

Pay ONLY these rates and NOT a Lire more

Post-war euphoria. A tariff for gondolas in Venice.

June 11th

Brigadier Edwards stayed the night at the 98th General Hospital on his way to Greece. He told us that the hospital is to remain in Bari in order to treat any injuries our troops may sustain, and only when they have been released from service will the hospital close.

He also asked me to volunteer for service in the Far East as officer commanding No. 4 Surgical Chest Team, and that if I did not volunteer he would order me to accept it. So there was no alternative. I was to spend the next few weeks preparing the necessary equipment, and persuading some of the personnel of the 98th General to go with me.

Fortunately, on August 14th, Japan surrendered, and I was told that I should be sent to Rome, to command the surgical division of 104 General Hospital with the rank of Lieut. Colonel.

August 25th

I was allowed one month's home leave. I had been abroad for almost three years, but when I returned home to my parents and family I felt as though I had been away no longer than a month. The leave period passed too quickly and I was soon on the train again passing through France to Italy.

December 17th

I reported to the 104th General Hospital, which was housed in a school very near to the Lateran Palace. I was not very busy. We had a few chronic infected

Two extremes — medical personnel 'swanning' in Austria. Extreme left is Maj Ivor Lewis, who played rugby for England. Extreme right, Geoffrey Wooler who was, he recalls from schooldays (page 5), hopeless at rugger.

wounds that were progressing well and could have been evacuated at any time, otherwise there was little else to do, except to explore the Eternal City.

At Christmas I went to an officers' leave hotel in Alatri for a few days, and in January I spent a week at the Cristallo Palace hotel in Cortina trying to ski. Cortina d'Ajurpezzo being one of the main tourist attractions in Italy, and especially for winter sports, all the hotels had been requisitioned. They were full of personnel from all services enjoying a holiday and most of them trying skating and skiing for the first time.

Everybody was having 'a go' at doing something in the snow. However there were so many accidents that the army had to send a 200 bedded hospital to Cortina to deal solely with orthopaedic cases, fractured leg bones being a daily occurrence.

Back at the 104th Gen. Hosp. in Rome I received notification that I should be released from the army in February so I had only a few weeks left to wait.

On two occasions Princess Doria-Pamphilj invited me to lunch and I also attended a musical soirée at their home. The Prince was educated at Magdalen College, Cambridge. He had a sculling accident and while he was being treated in England he fell in love with and married his nurse who was a Scot. It was a very happy marriage, for she supported him loyally with love and affection throughout the whole of his difficult life.

Prince Doria did not agree with dictators and soon quarrelled with Mussolini. When Mussolini conquered Abyssinia, the Palazzo Doria in the Corso was the only building without a flag to celebrate victory. The Prince was sent to an imprisonment camp at Arezzo, but this only strengthened his resolve.

Later, when the war came, Prince Doria, who had been freed again, received a short warning that the Germans suspected him of criminal activity, and were going to arrest him. The Princess and their daughter dyed their hair and sought shelter in the poorer parts of Rome.

The Prince remained in his house and when the Germans forced an entry, he had just time to hide in a secret room known only to the family since the Palace was built, which certainly saved Prince Doria's life.

After Rome was liberated and it was safe for the Dorias to return home, Prince Doria asked his daughter Orietta to dance with him. The two waltzed around the magnificently gilded ballroom, a wonderful way to express their joy at being free and together again.

The allies asked Prince Doria to be mayor of Rome — the first after its liberation. He addressed the Romans in the Town Hall and this is what he said: 'Let us remember that the word "Liberty", if it is to achieve its true meaning and efficiency, and be to the benefit of all, we must add the words "Duty" and "Responsibility". We must attempt to keep alive in our hearts a spirit of brotherly charity to one another, we must feel compassion for he who suffers, and aid him in need. We must be honest and upright in the performance of our duties, may they be public or private, and we must help one another to support the inevitable difficulties of the moment, and finally, "Let us love one another".'

January, 1946

When I returned to Rome from Cortina, I was informed that as soon as a replacement could be found I should be sent home on leave and later released from the army. This could happen any day, so I went to say goodbye to the Dorias.

Prince Doria entrusted me with a letter which he requested me to take to his sister-in-law who was living in Kent. The Italian postal service had not yet commenced to function properly.

Train loads of troops were leaving daily. I spent my remaining few days going through all the photographs I had taken and labelling each one. I counted

Homeward bound.

2,300. I entered a photographic competition and won the 4th prize for the ones I had taken of the Uffizi Galleries in Florence. I obtained two ammunition boxes made of steel in which I packed my photographs and other important things. After painting on the boxes my home address, I took them to Rome Central Station for dispatch to England.

On February 3rd I had my final medical examination and was certified as free from infection, and on February 19th left Rome by train for London.

I was granted ninety five days home leave with pay and 'released from embodied service' on May 25th, 1946. I had served six years nine months in active service and felt I needed a rest.

By the KING'S Order the name of

Major G. H. Wooler,

Royal Army Medical Corps,

was published in the London Gazette on

29 November, 1945,

as mentioned in a Despatch for distinguished service.

I am charged to record

His Majesty's high appreciation.

J. J. Lawson

Secretary of State for War

10

Back in Civilian Life

During my service I had had an enormous surgical experience which was exciting at first, but to see hundreds of young men mutilated in their prime of life became mentally exhausting. I tried not to show it and only when the war was over did I react by thinking that I had had enough surgery and would never be able to achieve anything surgically again.

In this state I went home to my parents, who hardly mentioned the war but only the future, which was good for my morale. My brother, Loy, who had been serving in the Royal Artillery, had married an officer in the ATS while in Devon. They had a son, Peter, when I returned home. I had not seen my brother nor my sister, Joyce, for nearly four years, so it was interesting to hear of some of their experiences while I was serving abroad.

In 1945 Loy was commanding an A.A. Battery at Dover when his radar equipment registered a German plane going absolutely in a straight line, which he had never seen before. A number of German fighter planes were accompanying the straight line object, threatening our coastal defences, but my brother ignored these fighter planes and fired all his guns at the straight line object and miraculously it came down in a field almost intact. It was a V1 missile. Nearly everybody from the War Office arrived to see it the next day and my brother was awarded an MBE.

My sister had worked at Harewood House with a Voluntary Aid Detachment. One day, when she was arriving in her car, she met a lady walking towards the house carrying a large basket. Thinking she was a land girl because she wore an old mackintosh and rubber boots, she offered her a lift, which was glady accepted by the Princess Royal.

The encouragement from my parents, and living in Shadwell village away from all previous turmoil, soon restored my confidence, and in less than a month I wanted to commence work again.

Returning to the London Hospital I found there were many opportunities waiting for me. Mr. Charles Keogh, now Head of the Department of Ear, Nose and Throat Surgery, offered me a Consultant post with him. Mr. Frederick

Herbert Bentley O.B.E, who had just been appointed Professor of Surgery at Newcastle, offered me another Consultant post as Assistant Professor in his unit. But I had become interested in thoracic surgery so I went to see Tudor Edwards at his home, 139 Harley Street. He was delighted when he heard my intentions and particularly because he had not influenced me in any way himself. (He certainly had not persuaded me to make this decision). I was immediately appointed his Surgical First Assistant.

Mr. Russell Howard had died in 1942 and had been succeeded by Mr. George Neligan who was now the Senior Consulting General Surgeon at the London Hospital. He too was anxious to receive my services, and after discussing the matter with Mr. Tudor Edwards, they agreed that I could hold two Surgical First Assistantships at the same time, one with Tudor Edwards and the other with George Neligan.

It became obvious that Tudor was not well; he had had a second coronary thrombosis while I was serving abroad, which had weakened him considerably. When he was in London he spent every Sunday resting in bed at his home. Lord Evans always went to see him and cheered him up by telling him the hospital gossip. In order to lessen his workload, Mr. Vernon Thompson had been appointed a Junior Thoracic Surgical Consultant.

Tudor and his brother-in-law, Dr. Jenner Hoskins, both had houses in Trebetherick, North Cornwall, where they all went for the summer holidays in 1946. In early August Mrs. Tudor telephoned me at the London Hospital and invited me to stay with them for a few days. The next morning I received a letter confirming this invitation.

On Friday evening, August 16th, I telephoned to say that I could come on Sunday but, because of my commitments at the London Hospital, would not be able to stay longer than two days. Tudor then took over the telephone, saying that two days was not enough and he wanted me to stay at least a week.

I had a small Morris 8 car which I prepared for the long journey but on Saturday evening Mrs. Tudor telephoned saying that her husband had died that afternoon on August 17th, 1946. It appears that she, Mrs. Tudor, Dr. Jenner Hoskins, his brother-in-law, and Margaret Hoskins his niece, went out all together for a picnic in the countryside with him. It was a glorious day and he enjoyed every moment, but when he returned home he became acutely ill. It was obvious that he had had a third coronary thrombosis. Jenner Hoskins was summoned, and he told Jenner that he had had enough and didn't wish to be rescusitated. So Jenner gave him morphia to relieve the pain and he passed away quietly.

The following week I was requested by the Chairman of the London Hospital to attend his funeral at Trebetherick and represent the hospital. Sir Gordon

Gordon-Taylor, President of the Royal College of Surgeons, telephoned me the next day saying that he was representing the College at the funeral, and asked me to accompany him. We agreed to meet in the evening at Paddington Station, and travel by sleeper to Plymouth, where a car from the Royal Naval Hospital, the Haslar, would collect us and take us to Cornwall. I arrived first at Paddington, booked a first class return ticket, but was informed that all the sleepers were completely full. I went to inspect the train, spoke to the steward in charge of the sleepers, gave him £1, and immediately obtained one. Then I returned to the ticket office where I saw Sir Gordon speaking to the clerk. They were arguing and so I went over to see if I could help. I heard Sir Gordon say 'I am Admiral Sir Gordon Gordon-Taylor' but this title appeared to have no effect at all, and he was told that all sleepers were still full and he couldn't have one. So I, having compassion on his age and seniority, gave him my sleeper ticket and returned to the steward, gave him another £1, and obtained a second berth for myself. We were met at Plymouth station by a Wren driving a Naval staff car from the Royal Haslar Hospital. I sat at the back of the car with Sir Gordon all the way from Plymouth to Trebetherick, and after the funeral back to Plymouth, he continued to give me a detailed account of Tudor's career.

After Tudor qualified he experienced considerable difficulty in obtaining a Consultant post. His parent hospital, Middlesex, turned him down, and his

The burial place of Tudor and Mrs Edwards, St Enodoc's Church, Trebetherick, Cornwall.

home town of Swansea would not accept him. Finally, he was appointed General Surgeon at Westminster Hospital but he was not allowed to do any thoracic surgery — it was a General Surgical appointment. Sir Gordon continued that fortunately at this time the Brompton Hospital, which to-day still calls itself a Hospital for the Diseases of the Chest, decided to embark on chest surgery and Tudor was appointed Surgeon to this Hospital. At last he was given a chance to practise his main interest. The surgeons he trained included Sir Clement Price-Thomas, who removed George VI's lung for cancer, Lord Brock, who was one of the most outstanding Presidents of the Royal College of Surgeons, Norman Barrett and many others. After his appointment at the Brompton Hospital, the tubercular sanatoria associated with the Brompton became interested in him, and he started another Surgical Unit at Midhurst Sanatorium with Sir Geoffrey Todd. Also, he paid monthly visits to a sanatorium near Montreux in Switzerland, but he was obliged to continue doing general surgery at the Westminster Hospital, which didn't interest him. In late 1936 the London Hospital offered him the opportunity to commence his own Thoracic Surgical Unit, which he gladly accepted, and immediately resigned from the Westminster Hospital. He had told me himself that the happiest time of his life was when he was given this opportunity at the London Hospital. Unfortunately, it was not for long, for in 1938, after returning in his Rolls Royce from Grenoble University where he had been given an Honorary MD, he suffered his first coronary thrombosis.

Life at the London without Tudor was not the same. My two Surgical Assistantships gave me considerable experience with civilian surgery and I started to publish some of my results. I also wrote a detailed account of my surgical experience during the War which gained me an MD degree at Cambridge University. I have mentioned before that the London Hospital was closely associated with the Royal Family. Queen Mary was our President, and staff from the Royal household were frequently admitted for treatment inside the wards. One day Queen Mary arrived at the Hospital to see a cook from Sandringham House who had had an operation. As she was escorted down the ward, she noticed that some patients had tubes coming out of their chests connected to bottles under the bed, and asked what was the matter with them. Now King George V had developed an abscess in his chest following pneumonia. He had a short tube put in to drain this abscess, but it never worked properly. At the Thanksgiving Service for his recovery in Westminster Abbey his tube was still dribbling pus into a dressing. When Queen Mary was told that the tubes were draining abscesses inside the chest, she asked why her husband had not had a long tube connected to a bottle. I wanted to say it was because he had been to

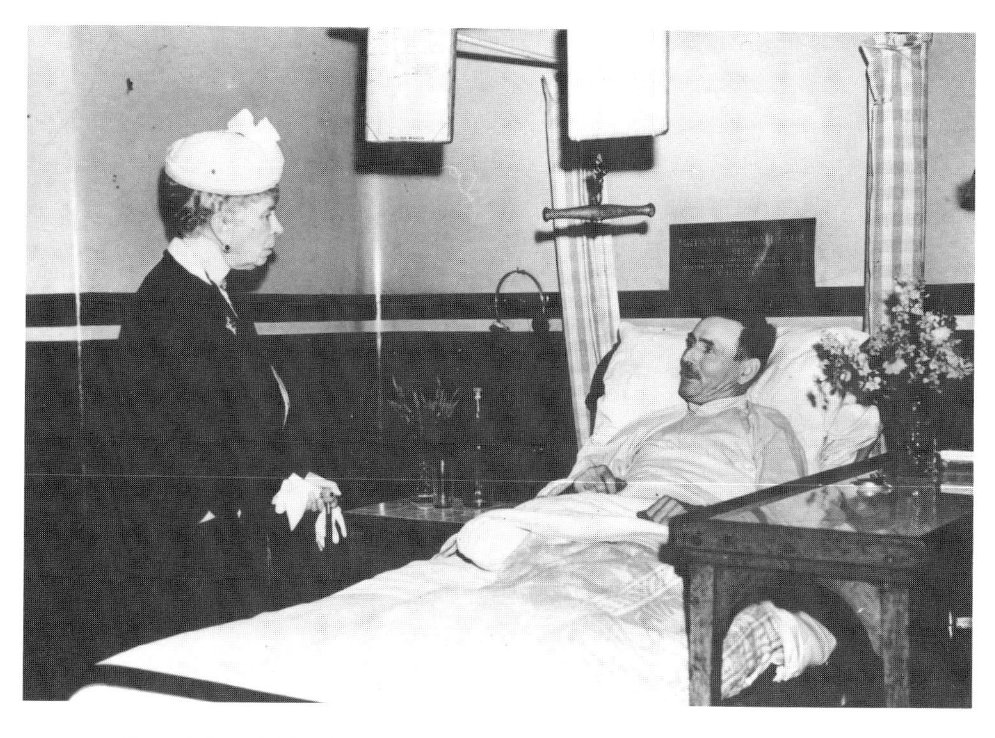

Queen Mary visiting the wards of the London Hospital on the 10th July 1945.

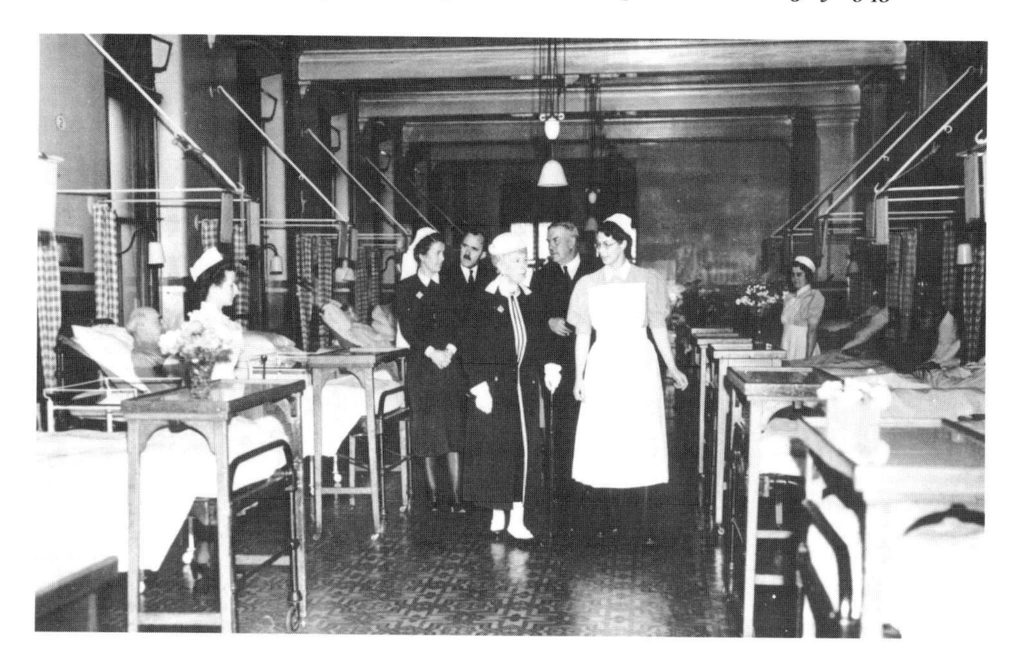

the wrong surgeon but being tactful I explained that some cases did not require a long tube. The Queen then went on past the Sisters' room into an adjoining ward and on the way noticed a kettle which was boiling and asked who was responsible for it. A young probationer nurse admitted it was hers, which prompted the Queen to demand: 'Turn it off at once, you are wasting the gas'.

The medical profession benefits considerably if the Monarch is a heavy smoker as, indeed, was King George VI. This habit in Royalty produces a windfall of civil decorations. When he was Duke of York he developed a duodenal ulcer which was successfully operated on by James Walton, Surgeon at the London Hospital, who was Knighted. Later on, after his Coronation, he started having difficulty in walking due to thickening of the arteries in his legs. Professor James Paterson Ross of St. Bartholomew's Hospital, London, and Professor James Learmouth of Edinburgh Royal Infirmary operated on him, and both were Knighted. One summer he started to cough up blood and went to Scotland to have a rest at Balmoral. The local G.P. there diagnosed that he had lung cancer, so he returned to London; Clement Price-Thomas of the Brompton Hospital removed a lung and he was Knighted. Finally, the King had a coronary thrombosis but unfortunately died before he was able to create yet another Knight.

One day in October, 1946, Mr. John Latchmore came to see me in London. He was the only consulting surgeon I knew well at the Leeds General Infirmary because during the War we had worked together on many occasions. He brought with him a message from Philip Allison, who was starting to do thoracic surgery in Leeds, asking if I were interested in joining him as his assistant and saying he would like to meet me in London on his next visit. We arranged to meet one evening at Oddenino's Bar. Philip said he was anxious for me to join him as a lecturer in thoracic surgery and after a short period he would advertise a Consultant post which, if I was working in Leeds, I should obviously have a good chance of obtaining. I told him that nothing would please me more than coming to work in the city where I was born, but first I must discuss it with my Chief, who was Vernon Thompson. Vernon Thompson proved sympathetic towards me but said he did not think I should enjoy working in Leeds where I would be a stranger and, apart from John Latchmore, I knew none of the Consultant staff and none of the doctors in Yorkshire. He agreed to release me for about one year so that I could find out what life was like at the Leeds General Infirmary and if I didn't enjoy it he would find another appointment for me in London.

The winter of 1946 was one of the coldest on record. I remember attending a Command Performance at Covent Garden where everybody was wearing their winter coats because there was no heating in the Opera House. Driving back along the Whitechapel Road was like driving over the limestone pavements in North Yorkshire. The salt, which was supposed to melt the ice evenly, only melted where it was dropped, and then froze again, producing holes in the ice. The road would have been better without the salt, so leaving a smooth surface to drive over. The AA kept me informed about the A1 road and when I was assured that it was open, I packed my belongings in the Morris 8, said good-bye to all my friends, who firmly believed I would be back soon, and then drove slowly to Leeds.

I began work in the General Infirmary in Leeds in February, 1947. Mr. Allison's Unit in Leeds was amazing — covering an enormous number of different conditions which certainly could not all be classified as purely thoracic. In London, a Consultant in thoracic surgery was obliged to confine his activities to the chest, but not so in Leeds, where the rule seemed to be that by commencing with a small chest incision you were permitted to extend it as far as you wished. Indeed, the full extent would give you access to the anatomy of the whole body. On one occasion I saw the top of the urinary bladder removed by the so-called Leeds incision. Fortunately, wounds do not heal lengthways commencing at the ends but heal across, one side of the wound joining the other. Long incisions, sutured properly, heal just as quickly as small ones. After I had been in Leeds for about six months, Mr. Vernon Thompson invited me to dine with him at his house in Wimpole Street, the intention being to find out if I was happy working in Yorkshire. Vernon Thompson was a first-class surgeon but he never enjoyed carrying out long, difficult procedures, so when I told him that I had been dealing with cases of cancer of the stomach, and that each operation took about six hours, his remark was 'How frightful'. I enjoyed the work in Leeds immensely. It was really general surgery with thoracic implications, and it was so varied you could never be bored. The following year in 1948 the Consultant post was advertised and I was accepted. At long last, after being away from home since I was thirteen years old, I was able to live again with my parents. My appointment allowed Philip Allison to travel and fulfil many invitations to lecture abroad about the work in Leeds. He flew to Nairobi in one of the early Comets. He was fortunate not to be on the same plane during its next flight because it crashed into the sea near Italy, the cause later being found to be metal fatigue.

The British Council invited him to lecture in Mexico City which required a visa. The British Council official met him at the airport but he was detained by the Police. His visa had been signed by someone who had been defeated in a recent Revolution and this person was now in prison. The official took the passport to be corrected, but he was away so long that Mr. Allison wandered into a cafe to refresh himself. The Police, thinking he was trying to escape, arrested him and locked him up in a detention room. Finally, the corrected visa arrived and he was allowed to go to the University an hour late for the lecture. There were only three people in the audience, a monk and two bearded surgeons. Philip doubted whether any of them knew what he was talking about.

His Outpatient Clinic was at the Leeds Infirmary on Thursday mornings. He escorted me there and showed me a room where I could interview patients. My third patient was a well-dressed lady who told me that her main complaint was that she had a bad 'peff'. Thinking this was a smell, I changed the subject quickly so as not to embarrass her. However, the next patient was an elderly gentleman, and he too complained of a 'peff'. This really puzzled me, and I wondered if it were common to all Yorkshire people. I went into the next room to ask Mr. Allison what was meant by a 'peff'. He comforted me when he explained that it was a Yorkshire expression for a dry, unproductive cough and had nothing to do with smell.

Mr. Allison was meticulous about cleanliness in his operating theatre. He and his assistants would change all their clothing before scrubbing up. Visitors were obliged to cover completely in clean cotton gowns, wear cotton boots etc. only their eyes and hands being visible. Nobody was ever allowed to cough or sneeze when an operation was in progress. His theatre porter was a man called Foulds, who, like the visitors, was always correctly attired before entering to work in the theatre.

One Tuesday morning Professor Grey Turner from Newcastle came to see Philip operate. He was an elderly gentleman with a longstanding international reputation. I saw Mr. Allison look irritated as the visitor entered the theatre, his gown unfastened, his mask not covering his nose, and a lot of loose hair escaping from beneath his linen cap. The operation was one with a really long incision commencing behind the shoulder blade and extending down obliquely almost as far as the navel. The other visitors drew aside so that the eminent Professor Grey Turner had a good view. I thought he must be short-sighted when I saw his head only inches away from the large open wound. Mr. Allison was obviously becoming more disturbed, and did not know how to deal with so eminent a person until the Professor actually coughed into the wound. Philip Allison put down his instruments, looked across the theatre at his theatre porter and shouted: 'Foulds, get out and never cough in my theatre again'. 'Yes sir', was the answer, and he had no more trouble with the Professor.

In 1947 the International Society of Surgeons held a meeting in London. This was an emotional experience for everyone, taking place in the bombed

Royal College, and in a City that had experienced over four years of war. Delegates came from all over the world to see London and to meet their surgical friends. The honour of presenting the first paper was given to Professor Renée Leriche, an elderly surgeon from Paris who had served in both World Wars. John Borrie, a New Zealand surgeon, was sitting next to Professor Alf Blalock at this opening session, Blalock being one of the most eminent American surgeons, who had had considerable success operating on blue babies. Renée Leriche spoke slowly in French, using his whole body to emphasise important points by moving his arms and legs, behaving rather like a ballet dancer. John Borrie, who could not speak French, noticed that Alf Blalock was laughing, so asked him if he could understand. Blalock replied: 'No, not a word, but boy isn't it good?'

Two surgeons from Malmo in Sweden called to see us in Leeds on their way to a meeting in London which I was attending myself, so I offered to take them in my car. On the way to London they expressed the wish to see a surgeon's house in Harley Street, if I knew of somebody who would not mind being disturbed. No. 139 Harley Street had been sold to an elderly, retired physician called Sir Alun Rowlands after Mrs. Tudor Edwards had died. He had taught me when I was a student at the London Hospital so I knew him fairly well and did not think he would mind my bringing two surgical colleagues from Sweden to meet him. Tudor's former secretary, Miss Harvey, opened the door and escorted us into the dining room which was being used as a waiting room. Sir Alun soon entered and while introducing him to the two visitors, I did not realise that he was almost completely deaf. Miss Harvey should have warned me, but he quietly thanked me for bringing him two private patients and requested them to go one at a time into his consulting room to be examined. I had to shout loudly in order to make him understand the position and my shouting brought Miss Harvey back into the room. With her help we explained that they had not come to be examined themselves but to examine his house. He was amused and conducted us around the house and invited us to tea with him.

In April, 1953, Sir Anthony Eden, our Foreign Secretary, was having attacks of abdominal pain caused by gallstones. Lord Evans, his physician, advised him to have his gall bladder removed. One of my friends, Guy Blackburn, assisted at the operation, which did not go as planned. The Press reported that Eden continued to run a temperature, and bile was leaking from the wound. Soon after this episode, I met Guy Blackburn in London so I asked him what really had happened at the first operation. He told me that the surgeon had removed the gall bladder through a very small incision which did not allow him to see the anatomy correctly and unfortunately he divided the main bile duct from the liver. A second operation had failed to repair the damage. Some days later, while I was dining with Lord Evans, I learnt the remainder of this story. By sheer good fortune, at the time that Eden was ill, a Dr. Cattal from Boston, Mass., came to London to give a lecture at the Royal College of Surgeons on 'Injuries to and repair of the common bile duct'. He had had more experience of this condition that any other surgeon in the Western World. Lord Evans seized the opportunity for Dr. Cattal to meet and examine Sir Anthony. He confirmed that reconstruction of the common bile duct was necessary in order to save his life. Dr. Cattal added that he would gladly do this for him. But the problem now was the publicity which would erupt when the press realised that because the British Foreign Secretary had had a bad operation in Britain, it was necessary for an American to correct it . Lord Evans told Dr. Cattal that it was important to inform the Prime Minister and obtain his consent. An appointment was made for both of them to speak to Sir Winston Churchill at 10 Downing Street.

On the way, Dr. Cattal became very nervous at the thought of having to see the 'great man' and when they entered 10 Downing Street he was in a real state of agitation. Horace Evans comforted him, saying that he would do most of the talking, but Churchill wanted to find out about Dr. Cattal — what his capabilities were, etc — so asked him how many similar cases he had operated on, and had they all been successful. Finally, Churchill agreed to Cattal operating, on condition that the operation was performed in London; which annoyed Dr. Cattal immensely. Looking firmly at Churchill, thumping the desk with his hand, he said: 'No, Sir, either he comes to me in Boston or I do not operate'. Churchill hesitated for what seemed to be a very long time, then replied that he would allow Eden to go to Boston, where the operation was successfully performed.

11

Open Heart Surgery

In 1954 the Leeds University decided to create a full time Professorial Unit in Medicine and a similar one in Surgery. Sir Ronald Tunbridge accepted the appointment of Professor of Medicine. Mr. Philip Allison was obviously the most suitable choice to be Professor of Surgery but when he asked to see the Vice Chancellor about this appointment, he was informed that it was definitely full time and he would not be allowed to do any private work. Mr. Allison did not agree with this commitment, so the following year, 1955, he left Leeds to become Nuffield Professor of Surgery in Oxford. This was a mistake for him and for Leeds, because he was never really accepted in Oxford. His colleagues there, having qualified in Oxford or in London, spoke with a different accent, which irritated him. They certainly did not know the meaning of a 'peff'. He spent as much time as possible lecturing and operating abroad making full use of his sabbatical leave in order to get away from an environment he did not enjoy.

John Aylwin joined me at the Leeds Infirmary as a Consultant in Thoracic Surgery and I was put in charge of the Unit taking over all Philip Allison's commitments. Dr Roscyski was a Polish refugee working at Pinderfields Hospital, Wakefield, whom Philip Allison had created a Consultant Surgeon before leaving. I never found out whether this man had a medical qualification, he certainly was an amazing technician, being able to remove a lung in a few minutes, and extracting ribs like teeth. I think he was in his final year as a medical student in Poland when the War commenced, so he had no chance of finishing his examination to qualify. Technically he was amazing, and gave good service, provided you controlled what he was doing.

I had been interested for some time in liver cirrhosis. Dr. Sheila Sherlock sent me a few cases from Hammersmith Hospital which she considered required surgery. After the patients had returned to London I would visit Hammersmith Hospital to see how they were progressing. It was on one of these visits that I met Dr. Dennis Melrose. He was working in the Department of Physiology at Hammersmith, building a prototype heart/lung machine, the first one to be designed and built in Britain.

On a subsequent visit Dennis told me that the Nuffield Foundation had agreed to pay for the construction of three heart/lung machines similar to the prototype he had developed. The first one would go to Hammersmith Hospital where Bill Cleland was the Cardiac Surgeon. The second would be sent to Moscow and the third could come to Leeds if the necessary arrangements were made, because the machine was still regarded as being in the experimental stage.

Our main commitment was that we should co-operate closely with the Department of Physiology at the Leeds Medical School and they in turn would continue to advise us and supply us with dogs for experimental surgery. Only when the dogs survived surgery and looked in reasonable shape were we to start operating on humans. This proved to be an unsatisfactory arrangement. The Medical School could not supply us with a sufficient number of dogs, and on more than one occasion we discovered that post-operatively they were transfusing the dog we had just operated upon with blood that had been stored for over a week. It smelt bad, and when it was given, promptly killed the dog.

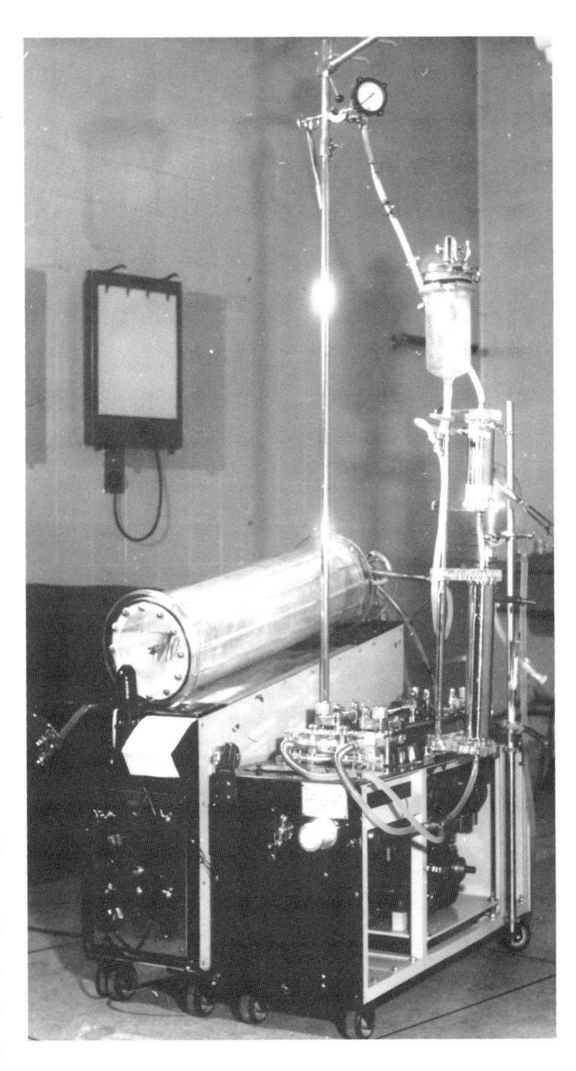

The third heart lung machine to be built in Britain, and the first in Leeds, designed by Dennis Melrose.

We heard of a dog dealer in Thirsk where we could buy them for a few pounds, so I bought a Bedford van and our theatre porter Leslie Catchpole, who was training to be a pump technician, went to Thirsk regularly to fetch the dogs when we required them.

The machine had arrived without any tubing or canulae to connect it to the patient's arteries and veins.

The blood would be in contact with the inside of the tubing and canulae where it was essential to have an absolutely smooth lumen. Any roughness would damage the blood cells.

Tubing and canulae with perfectly smooth interiors were unobtainable in Britain. I approached several engineering firms in Yorkshire to ask for their support, but they all refused. Finally a technician working in the Infirmary whose hobby was repairing antique clocks, said he could make the metal arterial canulae for us, and indeed he did.

My American friends sent over a generous consignment of plastic tubing and also the blueprints from the Mayo Clinic describing how they had made their metal canulae. Being able to use the correct equipment improved our work with dogs. Their survival was of paramount importance, nothing else mattered, which was certainly apparent one day when we had an ether explosion just as we were finishing a successful operation.

The anaesthetic apparatus, which we were using, belonged to the department of physiology and they serviced it for us. One of the technicians, when cleaning the machine, had inadvertently used static rubber tubing to replace the non-static type.

We were just finishing the operation when my anaesthetist heard a click near to the ether bottle, and without warning us he fled from the theatre, when there was a loud bang. The force threw both my house surgeon and my registrar on to the floor.

Dr. Peter Nixon, who was working the heart/lung machine, strode over the two bodies, taking no notice of them but saying, 'We must keep this dog alive'. My registrar looked up at him and remarked from the floor: "Ere, what about us?' Fortunately, nobody was injured, and the dog did survive.

At this time the Post Graduate School in Hammersmith and ourselves in Leeds were the only two cardio-surgical units in Britain using a heart/lung machine so we were in constant communication with the Hammersmith team. Together we decided that the machine was causing an unacceptable degree of haemolysis after a long perfusion. So Peter Nixon, the Research Fellow, spent two weeks at Hammersmith Hospital with Dennis Melrose and they decided to change the original bar pumps of the machine to the rotary type. We were almost a year adjusting the apparatus, training a team etc. before we started having a run of successes with the operations on dogs. Finally, in 1957, we took our equipment from the Medical School to the Leeds Infirmary to operate on humans. The first cases which the cardiologists referred to us for surgery were really in a terminal state of heart failure. Not only their heart but also their liver and kidneys were affected: trying to repair their heart was not enough. Losing our first two cases was a great disappointment, but we should not have accepted them for surgery. However, in February, 1957, we successfully repaired a leaking mitral valve in a woman aged forty one. On reflection we were very lucky because we had little equipment to perform this new type of surgery, as it was either not available or too expensive. For example, we had no mechanical respirator so if a patient required assistance post-operatively in order to breathe properly, we had to use the anaesthetic machine, squeezing the bag manually in order to inflate the patient's lungs. One patient I remember required this for five days and nights, the team working in shifts all this time. The work became so time consuming that the wives of two of the members of the team threatened divorce. I went to pacify them at their homes, because I did not wish to be responsible for breaking up families.

This new type of surgery was really a challenge which my team was determined to master. They paid no attention to how many hours they were supposed to work and never knew the time, only whether it was light or dark. Once I remember saying to them: 'You should go outside the hospital, to see what the outside world is like, perhaps the fashions have changed.' There was no doubt at all that the team enjoyed working together. I know only too well that when you enjoy what you are doing, you will succeed. We thought that our repair of the mitral heart valve in February, 1957, was the first case ever to be successful. We learned later that Merendino in the States had had a similar successful case to ours a few months earlier.

I was fortunate in having a number of business friends who were generous, enabling me to buy equipment instead of asking the various Committees for money, as by the time they had made a decision, the piece of equipment might well be out of date.

One of my great friends was Mr. Bernard Cayzer. He came to Leeds several times and took a great interest in what we were doing. He financed a Research Fellow for us, Dr. Peter Nixon. There was also sufficient money to enable the research fellow to have a part-time secretary. After about two years, the secretarial post became vacant and we advertised for a replacement. The applicants came to see me in my office with Dr. Nixon. One was an extremely attractive young lady, the wife of a physiotherapist, and was obviously our choice. We asked her whether she was willing to accept the position, first, she wanted to know why all the previous part-time secretaries had left within nine months. Peter Nixon with his hands in his trouser pockets, his paunch protruding above his trousers said 'Well, as a matter of fact, they all became pregnant.' I thought this was the end, but not so, she accepted the post and stayed with us for over two years. There was an element of truth in Peter's remark. The part-time appointment was highly suitable for a young woman who had just been married and if the marriage went as planned, the wife would have to leave before an addition arrived.

(Left to right) Sir George Martin, chairman of United Leeds Hospitals, with Christine Ionescu, Bernard Cayzer and Marian Ionescu at West Burton.

Our work was going well. We were having considerable success with repairing heart valves. When I noticed a swelling on the right side of my chest. Professor Goligher had two attempts at aspirating it and obtaining a biopsy, but proved nothing. As the swelling was becoming larger and difficult to hide by my clothes, I thought it might be a growth of the chest wall so I went to consult my friends at Hammersmith Hospital. Mr. Cleland operated on me removing a large tuberculus abscess between the two pectoral muscles. An x-ray of the chest showed a small tuberculous lesion at the apex of the right lung. I was referred to Dr. Scadding for treatment, who put me on the anti-tuberculous drugs to continue for at least two years. He told me also that in his opinion I should stop doing open heart surgery.

Before my illness, I had accepted an invitation to go to America as a travelling Professor which was financed by a Mr. Edward Ball. This necessitated operating and lecturing at three different Universities during a period of two weeks. I was really anxious to fulfil this engagement so I didn't mention it to Dr. Scadding. Three weeks after the operation I was on the French ship *La France* going to New York. I had chosen this way of travelling thinking that it would be more restful than going by air. The first evening on board I met two American widows, whose husbands had both been successful physicians and who were now spending some of their money. They joined me on every possible occasion, sharing a table with me and sitting in the lounge after meals discussing various topics. I was quite flattered at receiving all this attention and thought perhaps they needed male company. The last night on board I told them that I was going to Virginia University in Charlottesville. One of the ladies said that her nephew was in Charlottesville practising as a gynaecologist and that I really must meet him. I informed them that I was a thoracic surgeon, not particularly interested in things below the belt, so why must I meet him? The two ladies together in broad Texan accents said 'He would love to hear you talk'. I was flattered to learn that I had been a source of amusement for the whole journey. They were two grand ladies with an excellent sense of humour and I had enjoyed their company and their accent just as much as they had enjoyed mine.

I was worn out by the time I had finished the programme in the States and flew back to London in a Comet. Arriving in Leeds I went straight to bed and slept for almost four days.

I discussed the position with John Aylwin, my colleague, as to what I should do. He told me that he did not wish to become involved with the heart/lung machine but was willing to continue using hypothermia to correct the more simple lesions inside the heart. Our waiting list for heart valve surgery was enormous. Cases were coming from all over the world, including America, to

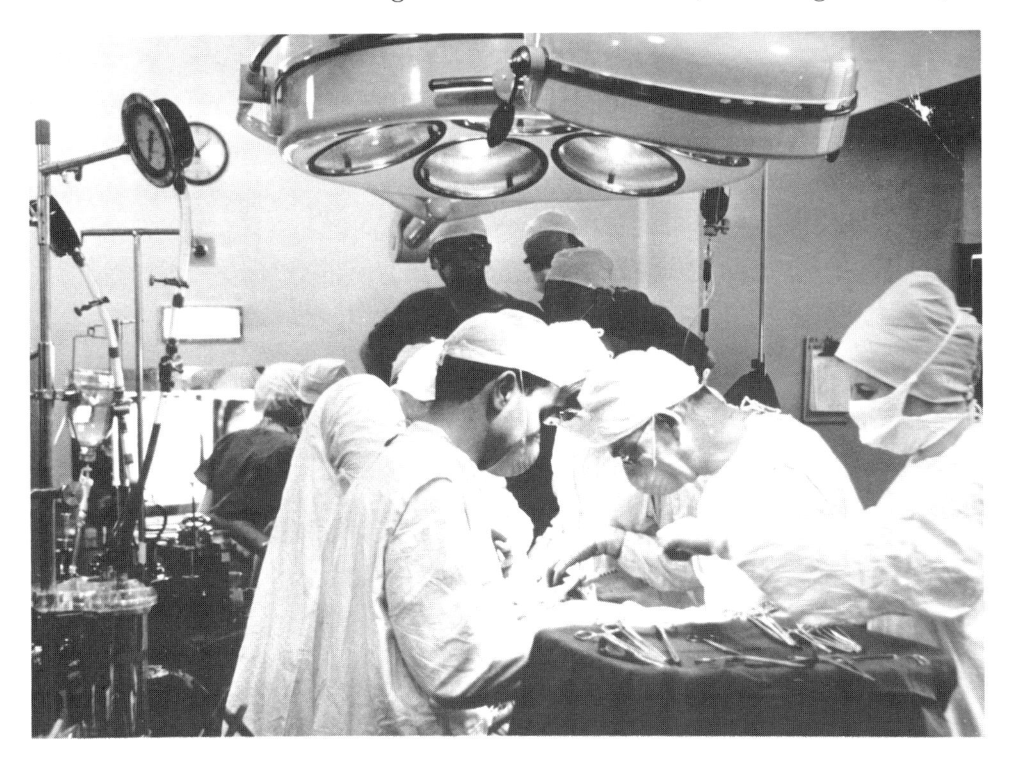

Operating at Leeds General Infirmary in 1968 — a heart valve repair. Geoffrey Wooler is second from the right.

have their valves repaired. Even if I were fit, there were really too many cases for me to deal with. We decided that a third Consultant should be appointed. At the next meeting of the Thoracic Surgical Society, of which I was the honorary secretary, I mentioned to a few senior members that Leeds had decided to make another Consultant whose main interest should be open heart surgery. I was amazed at the response. Three Surgical First Assistants approached me, for all of whom Consultant status was well overdue, but they were too precious for their respective chiefs to lose, so all three were immediately created Consultants and soon became internationally famous. I chose a young surgeon from the London Hospital, where I had trained myself.

My illness proved of use to the Thoracic Surgical community, for it was responsible for creating four new Consultants.

We had had our first successful mitral valve repair in February, 1957, and as our results improved, the cardiologists referred better risk cases to us. We were late in publishing these results because we were so busy, and had little time to sit down and write, but the news had spread, so we had many visitors from abroad, and we received innumerable invitations to speak at different meetings.

One of the earlier requests came from the Royal Society of Medicine at a time when we were still not out of trouble post-operatively. Driving to London with Peter Nixon in my car I asked his advice on how I should explain our mortality. He said it is quite simple, tell them you can repair the valve, but the boys can't keep them alive which was really true, because we had so little equipment to deal with the post-operative care successfully.

Soon after this meeting I was in Naples as co-Chairman of the Italian Surgical Society at their Annual Meeting. I was asked to speak about our cases at the end of the meeting, and summarize the different papers that had been presented. We had never tried to hide our own mortality rate and everyone knew that initially it had been considerable. This was the time when heart surgery was the fashion, it was exciting work and receiving considerable publicity in the newspapers so most of the Professors of Surgery in Italy looking for prestige 'had a a go'. At this meeting, each speaker competed with the previous one by quoting a smaller mortality, until the last Professor of Surgery from Milan stated his mortality for repairing the mitral valve was only 2%, which is about the same as taking out an appendix. At the end of the meeting, I summarized the different papers and explained how we had been repairing the valve in Leeds and then I continued, 'Gentlemen, I regard our life here on earth as only one part of our whole existence, in other words I believe in eternity, and with this belief I have no mortality.' The Neapolitan newspapers next day had the headlines, 'Professor Wooler believes in eternity and so has no mortality.'

"*There's no business like show business . . .*"

We're on the telly — a cartoon used in lectures. (© Telegraph Group Ltd, London, 1999)

Surprisingly, I was invited again to Naples to a Surgical Meeting sponsored by an Italian pharmaceutical firm. Donald Ross from Guy's Hospital and Chris Barnard from Cape Town were on the platform with me. The final banquet was held in the Capodimonte Museum, attended by the relatives of the Bowes Lyon family and the Mayor of Naples. Chris Barnard, with his film star good looks, had a crowd of young girls milling around him wherever he went, hoping to touch him or obtain his signature. The girls had followed him into the Museum but they had been kept in another room by the Police while we had our dinner. When the meal was over the Police allowed them to stay around the periphery of the banqueting hall, all of them looking at Chris the whole time, sighing, billing and cooing and making funny noises when he spoke, so that you could hardly tell what he was saying.

The previous year I had taken Chris on his first visit to Italy and we shared a room from time to time. When I got up to speak at the banquet to thank the Mayor and the pharmaceutical company which had sponsored the meeting, looking at the girls I said I thought they would be interested to know that I had slept with Chris, and continued 'I am sure if you were given the opportunity yourselves, you would not need to be asked twice, but I would like to warn you to prepare for a noisy night, because he talks in his sleep'. Chris shook his fist at me.

The Annual Meeting of the Thoracic Surgical Society was held in Leeds during my last year of office. I invited Dr. William Pickles, my friend from Aysgarth, as my guest. He was one of the old school, well into his seventies and preferred a stethoscope to any new mechanical device. Philip Allison flew over from America, where he had been working at Duke University, and brought an amusing film of a heart operation with him to show at the meeting. The film looked as though it was a true operation on a human, but actually it was farcical. Blood spurted out in every direction, blinding the surgeon and covering nearly everybody in the operating theatre, before a young surgeon stepped forward and stitched a small hole in the heart, which stopped any further loss. Dr. Pickles, thinking it was showing something useful, and not a farce, asked me if this happened with all open heart cases.

One day Dr. Phillippe Daumet, a surgeon in Paris and a good friend of mine, telephoned saying that he was housing a Romanian and his wife called Marian and Christine Ionescu. They had recently escaped from their country. He found Marian to be an outstanding surgeon but as his main interest was cardiac surgery, of which Daumet was doing very little, he thought he would be happier and more useful in Leeds. I flew over to see them. Daumet told me that the Ionescus had both qualified in Bucharest and later Marian was sent to America for a time to learn cardiac surgery. When he returned to Bucharest, he was provided with a large surgical unit equipped with spectacular and expensive equipment, a sort of showpiece for the Ceausescu regime so that visitors could see how advanced Romania was in heart surgery. The Government had really created a political gimmick and the unit remained under their tight control making it impossible for any normal person to work unhindered.

The Ionescus decided to leave. They asked the Romanian authorities for permission to go to Yugoslavia for just one day. When it was granted, they prepared their medical certificates and any other necessary papers and documents, then set off for Belgrade in a small Cinqua Cento car. First they went to the British Embassy to ask for asylum, which was refused. They received the same answer at the American Embassy, but the French Embassy issued them with a travel document, which was valid for three years and enabled them to visit all countries in the Western world. They drove to Paris, where Phillippe Daumet looked after them and found them some work in various hospitals with which he had connections. At dinner that evening they told me that they would like to spend a year in Britain and then emigrate to the States.

I was most impressed by speaking to them and Daumet told me that Marian was one of the best surgeons he had seen.

Returning to Leeds, I was determined to try and obtain appointments for them so that they could help me for at least a year before going to America. I spoke first to John Goligher, Professor of Surgery in Leeds, and he agreed to create a Lectureship in Thoracic Surgery, but without any salary, as he has no spare money. After considerable thought I went to see Mr. Arthur Holmes, a former patient of mine living in Pannal, near Harrogate. He was a wealthy businessman and proved to be most generous. Without going into too much detail, he immediately gave me a cheque for £20,000. This, with £10,000 a year coming from the Bernard Cayzer Trust Fund, was all I required. I converted the second floor of my house in Clarendon Road into a not very elegant flat for them. They arrived in their Cinqua Cento car which had a Bucharest registration number, and had certainly served them well. I was sorry later on when they changed it for a British car.

In America, and then in Bucharest, Marian had been dealing almost entirely with congenital heart lesions. I explained that my main success had been with diseased valves and I had an enormous number of cases on the waiting list. In fact, enough for two years without adding any new ones.

The weekends we spent together at my house in Wensleydale discussing how we could improve our valve surgery. We were hoping to be able to replace a completely diseased valve with something approaching a normal one and not a metallic prosthesis. I always went to bed first, but Marian would stay in my dining room reading and writing most of the night. He liked looking at the oak panelling, but he couldn't tolerate the clocks.

We were surprised when our new techniques in valve surgery were being published in a local evening paper, almost before the operation was completed. I received a warning letter from the General Medical Council accusing me of misconduct by advertising. We discovered that the leakage of information was coming from one of my theatre porters, who proved to be a reporter on a local newspaper who had applied and been accepted for a job at the Infirmary. I explained this to the GMC and there the matter rested. Attitudes subsequently softened and our work was widely publicised, notably by Frank Laws, who was a reporter on the *Yorkshire Evening Post.* Frank and I became friendly when I learned that he was reliable, accurate and trustworthy. He always insisted that his articles were read by myself and passed by the House Governor of the Leeds General Infirmary before allowing them to be published. It struck me as being rather stimulating that his other manifestation on the *Post* was as crime reporter.

Examining different tissue grafts for heart valve replacement with Dr Grimshaw (left) and Marian Ionescu.

Fortunately for us, the Ionescus enjoyed their work in Leeds and decided to stay. Marian took a degree and soon was made a Consultant in Cardio-thoracic surgery. Their fathers had died some time ago and after being away for over two years they wanted to see their mothers again. Both mothers were being watched fairly carefully in Bucharest because their children had absconded. Marian's brother was dismissed from his post at one of the main Teaching Hospitals as a reprisal, and sent to work at a small hospital in the country. I decided I would try to obtain permission for their two mothers to visit Leeds and so I arranged an appointment with their Embassy staff in Princes Gate, London. Arriving at the agreed time, I was ushered into a room and kept waiting for over an hour. Then a young man, smiling continuously, came to speak to me. He was called Ciubotaru, the name sounding to me like someone associated with Hiawatha. The main gist of our conversation was, 'Why had I come? why did not the Ionescus come themselves, etc'. I replied that I hoped he remembered the two Egyptians living in London who disagreed with the Nasser regime. They went to their Embassy pleading for their relations, and were never seen again. I knew this annoyed him, but he masked his feeling by producing a much bigger smile. Not wishing to delay my departure any longer, he ushered me to the entrance door saying he would request his government to let me know the answer within three months. Three months passed and nothing happened, so I went to the Embassy again; but achieved nothing except the advice that the Ionescus must present themselves at the Embassy and not keep sending me there. However, smiling, he said that he would contact Bucharest again, and see whether he could obtain an answer from his government.

A month later I was to speak at the Royal Society of Medicine so I telephoned Ciubotaru at his Embassy asking him to lunch with me at the R.A.C. in Pall Mall. He arrived in time, all smiles and over polite. At lunch he said it was essential for him to meet the Ionescus and if they wouldn't come to the Embassy could he meet them in a pub or some other address in London? I told him I would pass on the message. Just before we left the table he leaned across, looking at me, and said, 'You know, Mr. Wooler you cannot be a good surgeon without being a good Communist'. I was really furious at this remark and angrily told him I didn't know what a good Communist was, adding that first he had appeared to me to be reasonably intelligent, but now I considered him to be a damned fool. His smile disappeared immediately and I thought if he had a gun he would probably kill me. In complete silence he left the dining room, collected his coat and went straight out of the main entrance into Pall Mall. I hailed a taxi for him and he went away without looking at or thanking me.

Two gentlemen then approached me at the entrance to the Club, and showed me their credentials and badges: they were from MI5. We sat down to talk in a quiet corner of the Club lounge. I was asked how I got to know this man, etc. They told me he was the Fifth Secretary at the Embassy who had been sent to Britain to implicate refugees from Romania in espionage so Britain would expel them. The two gentlemen said that if the Ionescus were seen in a pub or anywhere in London meeting this man the British Intelligence would be informed in some roundabout way, and the Ionescus would be expelled from the country, presumably because they were accused of espionage.

That same evening Miss Alice Bacon, the Labour MP, came to dine with me and I told her the story. She knew all too well the activities of the Romanian Embassy, and confirmed the two MI5 gentlemen's advice, namely that the Ionescus must not in any way have contact with or see anybody from their Embassy. Since this episode with the Fifth Secretary I have always mistrusted anybody who continues to smile too much.

I was not going to give in too easily over the two mothers, so about two weeks later I went to seek advice from my friend Bill Deedes, now Lord Deedes, at the *Daily Telegraph*. He said he would contact his friend, Sir Alec Douglas

Home, about the affair. Sir Alec reacted quickly, spoke to the Romanian Ambassador and within ten days the two mothers arrived in Leeds. I was really so pleased, but not for long. Alas, a new problem arose. After arriving safely in Britain and being housed in their children's home, the two mothers soon had different ideas about cooking. The disagreement started slowly but gradually grew until there was almost a fight in the kitchen. My eighteen months' effort had ended in complete discord. It had been time consuming, and sometimes rather hazardous but, in a rather devious way, it had at least proved the old saying that it is unwise to put two cooks in the same kitchen, even when they have come from the other side of the Iron Curtain.

There is no perfect substitute for diseased heart valves. Marian and Christine Ionescu embarked on replacing them with biological tissue, using first pig valves, then later tissue taken from young calves. The Ionescus and indeed the whole team were absolutely dedicated, achieving excellent results.

In 1968 a Bradford lady underwent a six hour operation to replace three diseased heart valves with those from a pig.

Fortunately at that time my houseman's uncle was in charge of the abbatoir, and we were able to obtain as many pigs' hearts as we could carry. At the weekend we took them to West Burton, dissecting them on the kitchen table. The valves were removed and taken back to the Infirmary for sterilisation. The heart muscle was given to my friends in the village for dog meat.

The abbatoir floor was covered with fat and blood. The first time I went I did not realise how dangerous this was when wearing shoes with smooth rubber soles. I fell at least three times and made such a mess of my suit that I had to send my chauffeur for another one before I could return to the Infirmary in the Rolls with the pigs' anatomical parts.

I encouraged the team to continue and develop this work while I retired myself to the more simple lung and oesophageal surgery. Then I found that I had to wear spectacles when operating as I couldn't see so well and although this improved my vision I was conscious that it was certainly not as good as it used to be. When the spectacles were being changed almost every few months I thought that it would be better for me to retire. I had so many other interests to pursue which were denied me whilst I was a surgeon, so in 1974 I tendered my resignation from the Health Service. For the twenty five years of service I had given the Leeds Infirmary, as a reward I was presented with a cheque for £11.00.

12

The Woolton Affair

November 13th 1952

Mr. and Mrs. Burns, two friends from Dublin, were staying with me at my house in Clarendon Road. After lunch, we left in the Rolls Royce for the Annual Meeting of the Thoracic Surgical Society in Birmingham. My chauffeur, Philip Flaxinton, drove all the way. It was dark before we reached Birmingham and it was about 7.15 pm when we arrived at the Queens Hotel, where we had previously booked accommodation. Just after I had entered the hotel and before I had gone to my room I was told that Mr. Leslie Pyrah, the senior surgeon at the Leeds General Infirmary, was telephoning from the Belvedere Nursing Home in Scarborough, and wished to speak to me. I went to a call box in the main hall of the hotel. Leslie asked me to go as soon as possible to the Nursing Home in order to bronchoscope Lord Woolton. They considered he was dying of left ventricular failure and pulmonary oedema. Dr. John Towers, the senior physician at the Leeds General Infirmary, then spoke to me and reminded me of another patient I had bronchoscoped in an arm chair by his fireside: he had not had the strength to expectorate properly but aspirating his secretions with a bronchoscope relieved his breathing considerably. He wished me to do the same for Lord Woolton. I asked them to telephone the Leeds Infirmary, and to have a full bronchoscopy set ready for me. I also requested a set of instruments suitable for doing a rib resection and, most important of all, some food. I asked for these instruments because the daily reports in the Press strongly suggested that Lord Woolton had an abscess high up in his abdomen just below the diaphragm which so far had not been found.

I thought I should arrive in Leeds about midnight and be in Scarborough about 2.00 am. The manager of the Queens Hotel did not mind cancelling our rooms, and Philip and I ate together in the dining room. We had only time to have the meat course and coffee before we hurried away at about 8.15 pm. Just outside the city we filled up with petrol and oil. Philip was looking tired and I asked him how he felt. He didn't feel too good, and wondered if I could drive for a short time, so he went to sleep on the back seat of the car while I drove all the way to Leeds. We pulled up outside the Brotherton Wing of the Leeds Infirmary just after midnight. My instruments were ready as well as a few sandwiches and coffee, which were very welcome. I telephoned the Belvedere Nursing Home in Scarborough from the Infirmary and spoke to Mr. Arthur Watson, the surgeon on night duty. Everybody else had retired to bed. He told me that Lord Woolton was as comfortable as could be expected. He had been given something to help him sleep, and in his opinion it was a waste of my time going over. In fact, he thought it was quite unnecessary. I was a bit disappointed and explained that both Dr. Towers and Mr. Pyrah had asked for me to come and that all my instruments were packed in the car. He then replied that if Dr. Towers had asked me, he supposed I should go. Philip drove from Leeds to Scarborough and I took my turn sleeping on the back seat of the car. We arrived at the Belvedere Nursing Home about 2.30 am to find that another Rolls Royce had got there there before us, and I was greeted at the door by the Honourable Richard Dudley, brother of the Earl of Warwick, and secretary to the President of the Queen's Council, a position held by Lord Woolton at that time. He told me that he had already written Lord Woolton's obituary, which I thought was a bit premature and an unusual greeting. I told him that I hoped it would not be required, and Dr. Towers presented me to the other doctors present. They were Dr.Watson and Mr. Debenham from Scarborough Hospital, Leslie Pyrah, and lastly, Lord Woolton's private physician from London, Dr. Desmond Urwick. I looked a pretty dreadful sight, being unwashed and unshaven. I was wearing an old double-breasted grey flannel suit which never fitted me properly. Dr. Urwick on the other hand was immaculately turned out and spoke with a very affected Oxford accent. I think I was quite the youngest of the batch, and certainly looked it. Dr. Urwick couldn't understand why Dr. Towers had asked for somebody so young as I. In fact, I heard later that after he had been introduced to me, he went into the Matron's office saying: 'Who is this man, that has just come? Is he qualified?' However, I understood that I was accepted when he discovered that I was a Fellow of the Royal College of Surgeons.

We had a conference in a side room of the nursing home. Lord Woolton had been taken suddenly ill just before he was about to make his final speech winding up the Conservative Conference. He complained of abdominal pain and, although he was suffering considerably, he finished his speech and then collapsed. He was taken to the Belvedere Nursing Home, where he was seen by Mr. Debenham and Dr. Watson who summoned Mr. Pyrah from Leeds.

Thirty-six hours after the onset of pain, Mr. Pyrah removed a perforated appendix with general peritonitis. Lord Woolton's temperature never settled properly and a residual abscess was suspected. He was kept on antibiotics and three attempts were made to discover the abscess, but they all failed. A few days before my arrival, a twelfth consultant had been called to see Lord Woolton. He was Lord Horder, physician to the Royal Family. He concluded that Lord Woolton was dying of left ventricular failure and put him on drugs to improve his heart beat.

The X-rays were produced for me to see and they showed a grossly elevated right side of the diaphragm. Obviously something was pushing it up. I was then escorted by Dr. Urwick into Lord Woolton's room and was introduced to him. I must admit I felt a little nervous as I shook his hand, but he quickly put me at ease when he said: 'It is extremely kind of you to come and see me. Now you are in charge, tell me what you want me to do and I shall do it'.

I examined him: he was a very, very ill man. His rather protuberent abdomen was not easy to palpate but the most important sign was that his breath was fetid and smelled terribly which convinced me that he was coughing up a subphrenic abscess from the abdomen. We all retired into a side room to discuss what to do. I remarked that if indeed he was in left ventricular failure with pulmonary oedema, it was the first one I had come across which smelt of pus. I wanted to go across his chest to aspirate the abscess at once, but everybody restrained me saying I would infect his pleura. Then Dr. Urwick came into the room and in a loud voice like a Toast Master said 'His Lordship's pulse is 160, his temperature's 96° and his respiratory rate 46'. I stopped him wasting any more time and, patting him on his back, said 'Look here old man, you are trying to tell me that he is ill, and I can see it'. I went again to see Lord Woolton. He was deteriorating rapidly and nearly drowning in pus. The abscess had certainly ruptured though the diaphragm into his lungs. Without using an anaesthetic, not even a local, I stuck a large needle through the lower part of his chest and immediately withdrew thick foul smelling pus. At last, the other Consultants believed me, but it was almost too late because Lord Woolton then started to deteriorate rapidly. I was not sure whether to drain the abscess or to bronchoscope him first to try and clear his lungs of pus. Both Towers and Pyrah said drain the abscess. So I quickly did this while he was in bed, inserting a large tube which drained two pints of pus into the bottle I had brought with me. At this stage we really thought he was going to die, but after I bronchoscoped him, without any anaesthetic, and cleared both lungs of pus, his condition improved, and we put him on oxygen. I went back to the private room where previously we had had the conference. I had a cup of tea and was introduced to Roger, the patient's son. I went to see Lord Woolton again before leaving, and he had already improved considerably. I told him how important it was to breathe deeply and to cough when he felt he had something to bring up. He thanked me, shook my hand, full of gratitude, and so sincere, that I felt a lump in my throat and I think his eyes were moist.

He told me later when he had recovered, he really thought he was dying. I slept for three hours at the Grand Hotel and then returned to the Belvedere where Lady Woolton was waiting to speak to me. Unfortunately, the drainage tube had ceased to function, so I did his dressing, but was unable to persuade the tube to work properly. I surmised that it was being squashed between two ribs. I had only carried out an emergency operation and I must admit that I had never dealt with a subphrenic abscess in this way before. Neither had I heard of anyone else going through an intercostal space and diaphragm with a pair of scissors without any anaesthetic, but it had worked.

The next day I returned to Scarborough and while he was in bed, using only local anaesthetic, I removed a portion of a rib which enabled me to introduce a much larger tube into the abscess cavity. This continued to function properly until the abscess healed. Lord Woolton was discharged from the nursing home on December 18th. He travelled to London by train.

Early in the New Year I was asked to go and dine with the Wooltons in Brook Street, their London home. He told me that the Queen's secretary would be coming to see me because he had recommended me for a K. I am afraid this never materialised, and I was told later that it was turned down by the College of Surgeons. They thought the method I had used was dangerous and I was too young for such an honour.

Ex-Army surgeon saved Woolton

News Chronicle Reporter

LEEDS, Tuesday.

A BRILLIANT young ex-Army doctor saved the life of Lord Woolton with a last-minute operation, I learned tonight.

He is Mr. Geoffrey Hubert Wooler, 41-year-old thoracic surgeon at Leeds Infirmary.

He was called in when another Leeds surgeon, Mr. Leslie Nor-

MR. GEOFFREY WOOLER
He was mentioned in dispatches

man Pyrah, found complications in Lord Woolton's condition.

Lord Woolton, taken to a Scarborough nursing home on Oct. 11, when he collapsed at the Tory Party conference, had already been operated on three times.

Very delicate

Then, during a fourth operation, Mr. Pyrah found that only a further delicate and dangerous operation could save Lord Woolton's life.

It was all the more dangerous because of his low state of health.

Mr. Pyrah said he wanted a thoracic surgeon and Mr. Wooler was called from Leeds.

The operation took one and a quarter hours and was the turning point in Lord Woolton's illness.

Mr. Wooler, of Spencer House, Shadwell, Leeds, is assistant thoracic surgeon to the United Leeds Hospital Board.

R.A.M.C. man

During the war, in which he was a lieutenant-colonel in the R.A.M.C., he was mentioned in dispatches for his work with the surgical unit at Cassino.

Lord Woolton, now convalescing at his London home, is gaining strength rapidly and is making a complete recovery.

He is already able to get up for several hours a day, and to come downstairs for talks with his friends.

When he has recovered enough to undertake the journey he will go abroad for a spell in the sunshine before returning to Ministerial duties.

An Extract from the News Chronicle,
Wednesday January 21st. 1953

During the following year I had seven difficult cases similar to Lord Woolton's referred to me by Consultant General Surgeons. One was a particularly bad case. The abscess had ruptured into the chest and had destroyed the lower lobe of his right lung. It required removal of this lobe as well as draining of the abscess cavity, but all these cases made complete recoveries.

I wrote an article about them which I sent to the *British Journal of Surgery* for publication. This *Journal* is the main one for the Royal College, but the Editor refused to publish it; saying it was a bad method, and he did not agree with the technique. However, Mr. Norman Barrett, Editor of *Thorax*, published it for me in 1956. It created a great deal of interest and the requests for reprints of the article were quite overwhelming. I was also invited to speak about the method at two of the American Universities. I am glad to say that it has now been accepted as the best way of dealing with an abscess high up and behind the liver. In 1964, Professor Charles Rob and Lord Rodney Smith decided to include this method in their revised volumes on 'Clinical Surgery'. At the time, twelve years after the Woolton affair, my number of subphrenic abscess cases had reached over fifty. More surprisingly still, they had all survived.

My colleagues in Scarborough told me, after Lord Woolton had gone home, that if I had waited another hour and not taken a risk he would certainly have died.

The Wooltons invited me to London to see the ceremonies at the Queen's Coronation. I stayed at their home in Brook Street, London. It was a most enjoyable experience.

In the early morning of the great day Lord Woolton and his wife dressed up in their full regalia. He asked me to try on his decorative embroidered jacket which was a dreadful experience because it weighed about a ton. The weight of the waistcoat was like lead, and how he managed to stand wearing both the waistcoat and jacket I do not know. You certainly have to have a strong constitution to be an Earl. After breakfast the photographer arrived with all his numerous paraphernalia, so I retired upstairs to watch from the gallery. The butler answered the door and I heard the photographer request the butler to help to carry in his equipment. The butler was unaccustomed to such requests and, drawing himself up to a great height, he said: 'We have no spare manpower here' and then retired. Lord Woolton refused to allow me to go and help and, conducting me into his sitting room, he said: 'Let them sort it out themselves.'

Several months later I learned that the photographer was Nahum Baron on whom I had operated during the war in Italy. He had received an extensive shell wound to his left shoulder. He was the first person on whom I did a primary suture after excising the wound. Fortunately, it healed without becoming infected.

On the lawn at West Burton with Lord Woolton, 1958.

With Lord Woolton, Lady Woolton and Lord Hacking, 1963.

To see the Coronation procession, I was conducted to Selfridges in Oxford Street and given a central position at the front of the building just above the clock. The procession took a long time in arriving; but we did not suffer from either boredom or cramp because in a room behind where we were sitting there was more than adequate champagne and an excellent buffet lunch. It was altogether a wonderful day.

The Wooltons came every summer to stay with my father and myself at The Grange, West Burton, our retreat in Wensleydale. They loved the countryside and had known the Dales for a very long time. After they had become engaged and before they were married they both cycled to Aysgarth in Wensleydale. One evening, they stopped in Thoralby to seek accommodation for the night. The house, belonging to a Miss Smith, had a notice outside 'B & B'. However, when Miss Smith opened the door, and was told that they were not yet married, she agreed Maud could stay in the house but Fred had to look for accommodation elsewhere.

One summer when they were staying with us the front door bell rang. Lord Woolton answered it and on opening the door found Miss Alice Bacon MP had paid us a call. She was at that time Chairman of the Labour party, and Woolton Chairman of the Conservative party. Apparently my doorstep was the perfect place for political harmony.

My father and Lord Woolton had one interest in common and that was property, but my father, having suffered a severe stroke, was unable to speak properly, which did not prevent him from discussing various estates in Leeds. My father always took with him to West Burton a bevy of staff, his chauffeur, his cook and two valets. A nurse from Middleham was fetched each night to bath and look after him. When we were entertaining, I would engage a young man and his wife from Leeds, whom I knew well, to act as butler and housemaid. One weekend the wife arrived with her leg in plaster because she had broken her ankle, so her elderly mother came with her to help in the kitchen. All these people were living in the Grange when unfortunately my father became very ill. My father's cook had worked for him for many years and was devoted to him. To see him deteriorate so rapidly upset her considerably. She was, in fact, a chronic alcoholic, spending all her salary on gin. The butler's mother-in-law started having angina and was confined to her bed, and his wife with her leg in plaster was complaining of pain and swelling so she, too, took to her bed. My father's cook, seeing him rapidly deteriorating, took to her gin. During the night I heard a disturbance in the staff quarters and thought it was the two valets having a friendly fight, but next morning when I saw large blood stains down the second staircase I wondered whether somebody had been murdered. I traced the blood to the cook's room and found her lying on the floor in a semi-comatose condition, bleeding from a large gash in the thigh. She had fallen on a broken gin bottle. The Wooltons were already up and dressed so I went to speak to them. Lord Woolton, looking concerned, asked me what I should suggest. I thought the best solution was for me to return to Leeds with father, and ask Dr. Pickles from Aysgarth to come and send the remaining ill patients to hospital. When the house was free of everybody who was ill, my own housekeeper who lived in the village could come and organise everything for Fred and his wife. Dr. Pickles ordered three ambulances which lined up in front of the house, and as they were being loaded with stretchers, I heard one of the young lads from the village remark: 'It's only the Woolers, who have been having a house party'.

Just before this visit to West Burton, Lord Woolton had engaged a chauffeur who had previously worked for the Duke of Edinburgh. He was staying at the cottage of my gardener, so I suggested that he came to live in the house to help look after Fred and his wife. My housekeeper would cook, and perhaps he would wait on the table. I am afraid the arrangement did not last for long, my housekeeper did her job well, but the chauffeur was not accustomed to housework, so after a few days the Wooltons decided to return to London.

It was the start of a series of tragedies. My father only lasted three or four days and then passed away. His cook was admitted to Scotton Banks hospital and she never recovered properly and died from liver failure about a fortnight later.

Lady Woolton had complained of chest pains for a long time, but they were not thought to be too serious. However, the following winter she had a heart attack and soon went into left ventricular failure and died. Lord Woolton was left on his own. He came up to stay with me again the following summer bringing with him a friend of his wife's. She was a doctor called Lyn Jones. They had known one another all their lives; she was a charming lady, and a good pianist. Lord Woolton loved the Dales which he had known since he was a boy. They appeared to revive his youthful spirit. While he was sitting with Lyn on a seat near the waterfall in my garden he proposed to her and was accepted. I thought something exciting was happening, and did not know the cause until much later — after they had had a quiet wedding in London. His second marriage was also a success. They had many common interests and were devoted to one another. Later, when he developed a cancer, Lyn was a great comfort to him and helped him during the last period of his life.

The Wooltons had a country house at Walburton in Surrey. One weekend an agent from the Labour party came to stay in the village with the intention of finding something unpleasant about His Lordship, he being at that time Chairman of the Conservative party. The agent met Fred's butler in the local pub, stood him a drink; and then started to question him, asking whether he liked working for his Lordship and whether he was treated properly and so on. He enquired what the staff were having for dinner on this particular night, and was told it was cod. The agent then remarked that his Lordship would certainly be having salmon, which was quickly corrected by the butler because the Wooltons were both very fond of herrings, and always had them at least once a week. The agent asked no more questions.

Dinner at the Wooltons was always a ceremonial affair with gentlemen in dinner jackets and ladies showing their attractive evening dresses. Lord Woolton used to say that dressing properly for dinner kept the staff up to scratch.

I remember one evening at Brook Street the dining table was beautifully arranged with flowers, silver etc. The butler ceremoniously brought in the second course, placing a large silver salver in front of his Lordship; when he removed the lid, there were three herrings, one for each of us.

Lord Woolton told me something interesting which occurred one day at a meeting of the Cabinet. Winston Churchill commissioned an ex-schoolmaster called Mr. Park to inspect and report on our coastal defences and ports. Mr. Park had written a lengthy report and given it to Churchill. After reading the report, which more or less said that we had no defences at all, Winston decided to write another report himself. Mr. Park was summoned to the Cabinet meeting and given a copy of Winston's report. After reading it he was asked to sign it, but he went red in the face and his hands started to tremble and then when he had mustered sufficient courage he looked across the table at Mr. Churchill and he said: 'No, no, no, Mr. Churchill, I've never told a lie'. Winston got up from his chair, shook Mr. Park by the hand saying to him: 'Mr. Park tomorrow I am going on a long journey to Africa to see our troops and if I don't come back from that journey, when I reach heaven and speak to the Archangel Gabriel, I shall tell him that the last man I shook hands with on earth never told a lie, good-day Mr. Park'. When he had gone out of the room, Winston said: 'Tell that b b b not to come near me again'.

13
Arrested in Cairo

In 1971, I was invited to Cairo and given a first class ticket to travel by Egyptair. At Heathrow after boarding the plane which looked as though it had been well used, four men struggled up the gangway carrying a complete Austin engine which they put just behind the pilots' seats. I learned afterwards that it could not be housed in the luggage hold as it was much too heavy, but there was no limit to the amount of hand luggage, and so it was allowed to travel first class.

In Cairo I was taken to the new Sheraton Hotel. The Jordanian Premier and his retinue were also visiting Cairo and were staying at the same hotel. The day

Four pages — 25 milliemes

The Egyptian Gazette

92nd Year No. 29443 Monday, November 29, 1971

DAR ES SALAM every FRIDAY BOEING FAN JET LUXURY SERVICE ETHIOPIAN AIRLINES

GUNMEN ASSASSINATE JORDAN P.M. OUTSIDE THE SHERATON

HUSSEIN CALLS FOR 'FAITH AND NATIONAL UNITY'

KING HUSSEIN broke the news of Prime Minister Wasfy Tell's assassination to Jordanians last night in a personal radio broadcast at 8 p.m. (1800 GMT).

The broadcast, on official Amman radio, followed the reading of Koranic verses.

Speaking in low and measured tones, King Hussein said «We know this band of treachery and crime which was extended to assassinate our national unity.

«There can be only one answer to all these crimes. It is more faith and stronger adherence to national unity.»

King Hussein spoke for only two minutes.

An announcement by Amman radio said Jordan would go into mourning for seven days and the royal court announced palace mourning of 40 days.

The radio said all government offices and schools will be closed on Monday and Tuesday.

Salah

King Hussein said Foreign Minister Abdullah Salah was wounded in the attack.

He said El Sayed Tel perished «for the dignity of the homeland and so that our march should continue and our message remain high.

«I was on my way this afternoon to offer condolences (apparently for a Jordanian officer killed on Saturday night) when I received the shocking news of Wasfi Tell's death and Abdullah Salah having been wounded,» the King said.

4 envoys present credentials to Shafei

VICE-PRESIDENT HUSSEIN EL SHAFEI acting for President Anwar El Sadat, received the credentials of four new Ambassadors to Cairo at Abdin Palace yesterday morning.

They were the Ambassadors of Denmark, Algeria, Switzerland and Lebanon. ... Kield Vilhelm Mortensen, El Sayed Ibrahim El ... Mr. Hans-Karl ...

Sadat condemns crime in condolence message to King

4 PALESTINIANS HELD RESPONSIBLE — PLO DEPRECATES ASSASSINATION

JORDAN'S Prime Minister, El Sayed Wasfy Tell, was shot dead at the entrance to the Sheraton Hotel in Cairo yesterday.

Four Palestinian gunmen fired at him as he was walking into the Hotel surrounded by his guards after attending the morning session of the Arab Defence Council at the Arab League headquarters.

President Anwar el Sadat sent King Hussein a cable of condolences, condemning the crime on the soil of Egypt. The Official Spokesman expressed Egypt's regret at the painful incident.

El Sayed Zuheir Mohsen, member of the Palestine Liberation Organisation (PLO) Executive Committee, now in Cairo for the Arab Defence Council meetings, condemned the assassination of the Jordanian Prime Minister.

President Anwar El Sadat, in a message to H.M. King Hussein Ben Talal yesterday said: «I beg you to accept my regrets and the regrets of the Egyptian people for the crime which took place on Egyptian soil against your Prime Minister, the late El Sayed Wasfy El Tell.

«The Egyptian people strongly condemn such acts.

«It greatly pains the Egyptian nation that anyone should exploit its tolerance, its peaceful atmosphere and the safety offer...

WASFY TELL

HUSSEIN ...

ARAB DEFENCE MEETING POSTPONED
HASSUNA CABLES COUNCIL'S CONDOLENCES TO AMMAN

THE Arab Defence Council has postponed this morning's meeting to the evening, in view of the assassination of El Sayed Wasfy Tell, the Jordanian Prime Minister, and the absence of the Jordanian delegation.

This was announced by Arab League Assistant Secretary for Military Affairs, Major General Saad Eddin el Shazly, Chief-of-Staff of the Egyptian Armed Forces, after the conference's third meeting in camera yesterday.

GENERAL MOHAMED ... BARRE, President of the Supreme Revolutionary Council of the Somali Democratic Republic, left Cairo at 11 a.m. yesterday for home after a two-day official visit to the Arab Republic of Egypt.

He was seen off at the Airport by President Anwar el Sadat (Above picture). Also present at the Airport were Prime Minister Dr. Mahmud Fawzi, El Sayed Hafez Ismail, Adviser to the President for National Security, Ministers, high ranking officers of the Armed Forces, and Mr. Abdullah Ad... Ahmed the Somali Ambassador to Cairo.

The Jordanian Prime Minister was assasinated at the Sheraton Hotel, Cairo — Geoffrey Wooler felt it wise to move out shortly afterwards.

after my arrival, while the Jordanians were leaving the hotel, their Premier was shot and killed as he walked down the hotel steps. I was informed that a second Jordanian would receive the same fate if he could be found, so I moved across to the other side of the Nile to Shepheard's Hotel thinking it might be safer. I worked at the Maadi Hospital just outside Cairo. The first patient they presented to me for surgery was one of the fattest women I have ever seen. Every part of her anatomy was massive. She had been seen by a French surgeon previously who must have been terrified when he saw her because he refused to operate. However, she had a tight mitral heart valve and was coughing up blood so certainly required urgent surgery. I asked my Egyptian friends if I could bring over my anaesthetist for this occasion, for I realised that, even more than usual, the skill of the anaesthetist was going to be crucial. They gladly consented so I telephoned Dr. Grimshaw in Leeds and asked him to come over immediately. Fortunately, he arrived the following day and joined us just as we were wheeling the patient into the operating theatre. We had not warned him what to expect so when he saw the patient a tirade of oaths was thrown at us, every word unprintable in an English dictionary. Her body resembled a bag of fluid which was difficult to secure on the operating table. He wanted to leave immediately but we persuaded him to stay and with his help we managed to finish everything satisfactorily. The patient's husband was a Governor of an Egyptian province and he presented me with a fine silver coffee set as a reward.

My hosts very kindly showed me as much as possible of their country in the short time I was there. I was able to visit the pyramids, Luxor and the Nasser dam. The lake created by the new dam had unexpectedly yielded in a very short time an enormous quantity of fish. Fish was so plentiful and cheap that it was on the menu three times a day.

Dr. Tezarki, who had worked in America, was the consulting cardiac surgeon at the Maadi hospital, and had mastered the technique of open-heart surgery using the heart/lung machine. He requested me to return soon to operate on some patients having mainly valvular lesions, with which we had been reasonably successful in Leeds.

I returned to Cairo in May, 1972. This time I was kept extremely busy and had little or no spare time to see any more of their country. News of our exploits at the hospital spread rapidly so in the evening after the day's success, I was carried cheerfully by porters up the hotel steps; and after any failures, which fortunately were few, I was treated with politeness. On this second visit I had been so busy that I had had no time to do any shopping or even go out of Cairo. The last day I was there I wanted to see the villages in the country and something of the rural life. One of the French Embassy staff called Gerard, who was staying at Shepheard's with me, was to accompany me and, as he spoke Arabic, I was sure he would be of help. We both hailed a taxi and asked the driver to take us up the hills behind Cairo past the Mohammed Ali Mosque and the Citadel. I had an automatic focusing camera with me so I leaned out of the window of the taxi and took many photographs without asking the driver to stop. After about an hour we returned to Cairo and Gerard asked the driver to take us to the Souk because we wished to buy some presents. The driver was instructed to wait for us and we both entered the market. We were about half an hour completing our shopping. When we returned to our taxi, we found that there was a policeman sitting at the front with the driver. I thought that he had asked for a lift and that we were taking him back to the centre of Cairo, but after leaving the Souk, I noticed through the rear window of our taxi that there was a black Mercedes car continuing to follow us, with two men in it. I mentioned this fact to Gerard, who had more experience than I of Cairo, and he said that we were both under arrest. We were taken to the Police Headquarters, escorted upstairs and both locked in a room on the first floor. No explanation was given so I comforted Gerard by telling him that I knew the head of the Police in Cairo very well. I had successfully operated on one of his family and he spoke perfect English because he had joined the RAF during the second World War. I was relieved when the door opened and he came in escorted by two other officers. I asked him what the 'H' it was all about, so he explained. We had been seen photographing the hills behind Cairo, where, underground, there were the main storage tanks of petrol and oil. I told him that we were not interested in either petrol or oil, I wanted to have some photographs of the country people and their houses. If my photographs contained the site of these storage tanks, they would not be in focus. I had to surrender my film and then we were allowed to leave. We went outside to our taxi and found that the driver too was under arrest. He had been driving us without a licence for his car. I felt sorry for him, paid him, and gave him a generous tip. Gerard, understanding Arabic, told me that the driver had also been paid by the police for reporting on our activities so, presumably, what he had collected from the police and ourselves should have been sufficient to re-license the car.

In 1964 Dr. Peter Nixon, my cardiologist, and I were invited to go to Turkey and help them to commence open heart surgery using a heart/lung machine. It was several weeks before our commitments in Leeds allowed us to go, and in the meantime there had been a small rebellion in Istanbul. The army had taken away the Professors who had invited us and locked them up in a compound, recruiting young new Professors in their place. A few days before our arrival the newly-appointed young Professors thought that we would be very annoyed to see our original hosts living behind iron railings, so they were all allowed out. Both sides hated each other and each decided that we would not have the opportunity of telling the other any of our secrets, if indeed we had any.

We were met at the airport by a young doctor in a black Mercedes car, who took us across the Bosphorus through Scutari, past Florence Nightingale's hospital, then up into the mountains near to a skiing resort where there was a sanatorium. We were treated well but, we had obviously been kidnapped by the younger Professors. We were each given a room, which was rather primitive but clean. After washing and changing our clothes we were taken to the operating suite. It was well equipped but the heart/lung machine was packed in a box and had never been used since it arrived. I told them quite firmly that I would not operate with a machine that had not been tested properly. I suggested doing some animal experiments, commencing the following day.

With Siyami Ersek, a cardiac surgeon in Istanbul.

In England, animal experimental surgery is usually performed on dogs, but in Turkey they use goats. Having a certain amount of interest in cooking I could not help noticing that each time we did a goat experiment we had goat for lunch the following day, the taste perhaps being varied by the use of different herbs. The Turkish doctors said it was a shame to waste good meat and I must admit we enjoyed eating it, even though we were making a second acquaintance.

We had been confined to the sanatorium for three days and had seen nothing of Istanbul. One of the hospital workers who lived there offered to take us one evening in his car. After spending a few hours looking around the city, we tried to hitchhike our way back. This proved to be not easy. But after three lifts we eventually arrived at the sanatorium about 2.00 am. The gates were locked and firmly closed. Having some experience of such situations in Cambridge, it was decided that I, being the elder, would climb on to Peter Nixon's back, then when I was on the top of the gate I would pull him up after me. The plan worked beautifully, but at the other side we were confronted by the night watchman who had an enormous beard. He looked at us, then lifted up his beard and hidden under it was the most attractive large brass clock. He pointed to the time, it was 2.25 am. We both looked at our wrist watches, adjusted them, thanked him and walked away. He rewarded us with an enormous smile, and indeed he didn't forget this encounter, for when we returned to Turkey several months later he greeted us most warmly, lifting his beard again to show us the time.

The young doctors and their staff at the sanatorium were determined to succeed with open heart surgery before the older Professors could commence, for they were now back at work in the University of Istanbul. They begged me to operate on two patients before the end of the week, and they wanted as much publicity as possible. Fortunately, there was a great variety and a great number of patients requiring open heart surgery. I suggested to Peter Nixon to choose two patients with simple congenital lesions that could be corrected at normal temperature and which, if we were fast enough, would not require the assistance of the heart/lung machine. Peter selected two patients, one with a small hole in the heart and the second one with a partially closed heart valve. The television crews, the newspaper reporters, and all the media were invited to see the excitement which would provide two days of entertainment, for we decided to operate on only one patient each day. The patients were connected to the machine, and we were fast enough to complete the open heart operations before the machine had time to take over. The young Professors had succeeded, and received more than sufficient publicity to satisfy them; so we were then allowed to join the older generation in Istanbul. They housed us comfortably at the Park Hotel situated in the centre of the city. The next morning I was awakened at 7.00 am by somebody knocking on my door. Expecting to receive my morning cup of tea, I asked the visitor to come in. The door opened, and a tall gaunt gentleman dressed all in black, wearing an enormous headgear such as one sees on Egyptian gods, entered the room. He did not appear to be a threat and when he handed me his visiting card, I learned that he was the Patriach of Greece and had brought a blue baby for me to examine.

The child was five years old and possessed all the features of Fallot's tetralogy. I explained to the Patriach that full investigations would be required before a decision was made on whether or not surgery could be beneficial. I added that I should be pleased to admit the child to the Leeds General Infirmary, if the necessary arrangements could be made between the two governments. We shook hands and parted. I never heard any more about the child.

The last evening we were in Istanbul we were all invited to dinner at a restaurant for a farewell party. The young and old Professors attended as well as three Ministers of Health, the first of whom had been deposed at the time the old University Professors had lost their jobs, the second of whom was the present Minister, but was about to be deposed the following week, and replaced by the third. It sounded a faster turnover than we have in the British Cabinet. The two professorial sides disliked one another and conversation was a little strained during the meal. We were trying to keep the party going and under control, and everybody seemed reasonably happy until the belly dancers arrived. There was absolute silence at our table when the girls started to dance. The Dean of the University turned his head the other way and the older members obviously disapproved of the two attractive girls circling around our table. The absolute silence lasted for a few minutes. It was broken by Peter Nixon sitting at the other side saying to me in a loud voice: 'It's damn hard to keep looking at their faces'. Not everybody was amused.

14

The Manure Cart Taxi

When I was in Rome during the summer of 1961 Professor Pietro Valdoni invited me to dinner at his home in the via Carlo Fea. One of the guests was Gabor Petri, Professor of Surgery at the University of Szeged, Hungary. He was anxious to visit England, but in order to do so he required an official invitation stating that his English host would be responsible for his welfare while he was in this country. On returning to Leeds, I immediately sent Professor Petri an invitation asking him to stay at my house. He arrived here early in 1962 and after all too short a visit he invited me to see his unit in Szeged.

In September, 1962, I flew to Budapest with Andrew Hepper, my nephew. We were met at the airport by Professor Petri in a Russian car which he shared with the Professor of Medicine because they could not afford to buy one each. I sat on the rear seat with Andrew and about half way to Szeged, a Russian officer stood in the middle of the road demanding a lift. As we drew near to him he tried to stop the car and shook his fist, but our driver took no notice and managed to avoid hitting him. I looked through the rear window of the car after we had passed, and warned my friends that he had his hand on his revolver, but he did not take a shot at us so we arrived safely at Szeged.

I soon learned that the Hungarians hated the Russians for occupying their country and enforcing Communism. I noticed that when they took me into a restaurant, if there were Russian officers present, they would sit as far away as possible. Once they said to me: 'We want you to know that we can succeed in spite of Communism.' My first visit to Szeged in 1962 commenced a liaison and cemented a friendship which still continues today.

In May of 1964, on my way to Hungary, I first went to Korcula on the Dalmatian coast of Croatia to see how the alterations were progressing on a house which I had recently acquired. While in my house an elderly gentleman came to see me to ask if I wished to buy a second ruined house at the back of mine. I immediately agreed, because joining the two houses together would create a more comfortable abode, and greatly improve the ventilation. I could spend only two days in Korcula, then flew in a Dakota from Dubrovnik to

Belgrade. I have never experienced such an uncomfortable flight. Everybody was sick and I was too weak to stand when we reached Belgrade. A young Yugoslav had to hold me up by my collar and help me down the gangway. On the tarmac I was met by Professor Papo, surgeon to Marshall Tito, in full General's uniform who greeted me most warmly in spite of my appearance. I think I must have looked as if I had just been pulled out of the sea. I swore I would never fly again, certainly not in a Dakota, which seemed to have an attraction for air pockets.

The main reason for this journey was that I had been invited to operate and lecture in Szeged and Budapest. Papo told me that the day after tomorrow he was driving to Subotica and would take me with him. There I could take a diesel train to Horgos, and Horgos being only one mile from the frontier I could probably get a taxi to complete the journey. We telephoned my friends in Hungary asking them to meet me at the frontier at about 12 noon on the appointed day. Everything went according to plan as far as Horgos, but on leaving the station I found myself in a primitive village which looked deserted, no cars, certainly no taxis — only one or two horse-drawn carts passed me. I walked down the main street which was only dust and mud. I knocked on the door of the one house which looked inhabited. It was a farm. The farmer, who had just been 'mucking out', and his wife greeted me. The whole place had a pronounced farmyard smell, but fortunately the farmer spoke a little German so I was able to communicate with him. I asked whether there was a taxi or any form of vehicle which could take me to the frontier. He discussed the problem with his wife and decided he would take me himself, if I would wait for about half an hour. Then he disappeared. His wife roasted some fresh coffee beans, ground them and presented me with some excellent coffee. It was sign language with her because she spoke only Hungarian. After about half an hour the farmer re-appeared. He had apparently washed his cart but not himself. Fresh straw covered the back of the cart, and the bench on which I was invited to sit had straw on it, but the straw did not hide the smell which I am sure was pig manure because it was so overpowering. The cart had a central shaft intended for two horses, but the farmer had only one. My luggage was put in the rear and we both climbed up and sat down on the bench covered with straw and started our journey. The farmer spoke first, asking me when I was born and after discovering that we were both born on the same day in the same year, he would not stop caressing me; and I was firmly impregnated with his morning's work on the farm. Then he sang all the way to the frontier. About one hundred yards from the actual borderline he stopped and said he was not allowed to go any further. I paid him, dismounted, and walked to the frontier carrying my suitcase, wondering who was going to meet me. Then I saw two limousines parked under some trees and four gentlemen walking towards me, all immaculately dressed in dark suits. They found it hard to believe that the so-called important Professor from England had actually arrived on a manure cart, and at first did not know whether to take it seriously or as a joke but very soon we had a good laugh together.

My next visit to Szeged was in the following year. I had bought a three-litre Healey sports car in Leeds and I was most anxious to take it for a decent run. The European Cardiological Society meeting in Vienna had invited me to be co-Chairman and I wrote to my Hungarian friends informing them that I would be coming over by road after the Vienna meeting had finished, which was mid-day on a Saturday. To my great joy when I arrived in Vienna I found that my friend Bruno Paliaga had flown over from Rome. We stayed together at the same hotel and Bruno expressed the wish to accompany me to Szeged in my car. I had taken the precaution of obtaining a Hungarian visa before leaving England, but Bruno had not got one. We went to their Embassy, filled in the necessary forms and were told that granting a visa usually took three weeks; so I telephoned my Hungarian friends, one of whom was a member of their Parliament, and I was assured that Bruno's visa would be granted immediately. Bruno went daily to the Hungarian Embassy but no visa arrived. The medical conference ended at noon on the Saturday, and I had previously informed my Hungarian friends that I reckoned to arrive by car at their frontier about 4.00 pm with Bruno, but he still had no visa. I asked for a student from the University who could speak both English and Hungarian to accompany us to the Hungarian Embassy. It was an old Palace in the centre of Vienna and the gatehouse reminded me of one of the Cambridge Colleges, but it was not so elegant. Our student guide opened the door and told us to walk straight ahead. Two surprised guards tried to stop us but the guide said something to them and we were escorted into a waiting room at the rear of the Embassy. This was an extraordinary room, forty to fifty feet long and about fifteen feet wide. It had a very low arched ceiling and at least four office doors opened into it. We sat down and waited for half an hour. Then one hour passed. By two o'clock we were getting rather hungry so I asked our guide to go and buy some sandwiches and beer for us. He returned with a packet of sandwiches and a bottle of beer each. We had just finished our lunch when a male domestic cleaner came into the room and started to move all the furniture into another room. We were determined to hold on to our chairs so we sat firmly on them in a corner of the room. Then the servant rolled up the carpet and after he had emptied this long room of everything except our three chairs, he appeared

With (left to right) Joseph Imri, Prof Petri, Prof Kovacs and their wives.

with an electric sander to resurface the wooden parquet floor. This noise was absolutely terrific, and with the ceiling being so low it became quite unbearable. Bruno had not received his visa, and it seemed to us that the Embassy staff were creating a situation which was impossible for us to bear. I thought that now was the time for us to retaliate, so I did something which I have not done since I left school. I blew up my sandwich bag and burst it, producing a quite remarkable bang and an even more remarkable result. The servant with the sander had his back to us so he could not see our corner of the room. He jumped a foot into the air, and pushed an electric switch which turned off the current. Then he went out of the room returning with a screwdriver and started dismantling his machine. Two office doors opened and ladies came out to inspect whether the windows were still intact. We took the opportunity to ask them again whether Bruno's visa had arrived. The secretaries were becoming rather apprehensive of our presence and, within ten minutes of the bang episode, Bruno's permit was presented to us. The Viennese student always sent me greetings for Christmas addressing the card to the 'Professor who burst a bag.' There was no reason for any further delay, so we both set off for the Hungarian frontier and met our friends.

Crossing from one Eastern European country to another could be difficult, and probably the easiest way was to fly back to London and then fly out again to your destination. I never did this myself because I enjoyed travelling and meeting different people, but on one occasion I did regret that I had not taken the London route. In the summer of 1981 I was journeying from Korcula to Szeged in Hungary to attend a surgical meeting, and then returning to Korcula afterwards. Leaving Korcula I took the night train from Metkovic and shared a compartment with an elderly gentleman. We arrived in Mostar at about midnight, and thinking that we had the compartment to ourselves with one seat each, we started to bed down for the night. This was not for long; six gipsies entered our compartment. They took off their shoes and some of their filthy clothing; the smell they brought with them was quite unbelievable. To make matters worse they smoked and talked all night. I comforted myself thinking that if I ever were to go to heaven I should accustom myself to being with such people for they might be my companions. I used the window curtain to cover my nose and mouth. It acted as a sort of mask. The gipsy lady next to me looked about ninety. I had never seen such filthy feet. I thought she might be infested with fleas and I was nervous because I always attract them. However, I thought that perhaps gipsy fleas might behave the same as dog fleas, preferring their accustomed habitat. When we reached Subotica I discovered that I had completely lost my voice. It was probably a chemical laryngitis caused by the smell, the smoke and draught from the window which had to be open in order to survive. My Hungarian friends met me at Subotica and drove me to Szeged but I had no voice at all and could only speak in a whisper. Practically all the medical talent in Szeged was summoned to try and recover my voice. They produced sprays, gargles, steam and I don't know what else with no beneficial effect. Fortunately, I had brought with me a vast number of slides, which helped when I gave my talk, but it is the only time I have ever lectured in a whisper. I rested for a day in Szeged without any improvement, and then in the evening was driven by Gabor Kovacs back to Subotica with all my purchases and gifts including three frozen ducks, which were quite unobtainable in Korcula. This time I got into a compartment with two Yugoslav families who had four children. There was no room for any gipsies. The train left Subotica at 10.00 o'clock in the evening. The children were all under ten and were obviously excited at travelling by train and going to the sea for their holiday. Whether this in any way stimulated their reflexes, I do not know because in a very short time, all of them appeared to develop incontinence. Their parents were kept busy and soon ran out of nappies and clothing which they tried to dry hung on a make-shift clothes line across the compartment. The clothes did not dry fast enough, so the children ran about half naked for the remainder of the journey and kept climbing on to the seats. Their parents and myself were now busy trying to maintain some cleanliness of the seats which were being used as there were no dry napkins. The seat upholstery was a sort of plastic material which had no absorbent properties. I soon became wet myself, but the extraordinary thing is, I can now recommend child's urine as beneficial for laryngitis. My voice quickly returned, and before we reached our destination at the coast I was able to speak a few words of German.

When Professor Petri and I first met in 1962 he had asked me if I would accept some of his newly qualified doctors to work in Leeds for a year. A delegation from the Hungarian Embassy in London came to see me and I showed them around my wards explaining the type of surgery we were doing. I think the real reason for the visit was to make sure that I was not politically minded and would not try to indoctrinate them against Communism. A report was sent to their Government with the result that one young surgeon would be allowed to come; only when he returned to Hungary would a second surgeon be allowed out. Their wives and children had to stay. After the first two arrivals returned without trouble, subsequently, wives were allowed to join their husbands towards the last two weeks of their stay in Leeds. Altogether eighteen young Hungarian surgeons came to work each for a year with me in Leeds. The success of this arrangement with the Hungarian Government was entirely due to the efforts of Professor Petri. He was Rector of Szeged University, Professor of Surgery, and a member of the Hungarian Parliament, but he would never join the Communist Party. He accepted responsibility

With Prof Petri at the Royal College of Surgeons in London in 1984.

Receiving an honorary degree at Szeged University in Hungary.

for these doctors leaving their country to work here and he was to blame if they did not return. Only one of them absconded, and he did it in a clever way. Having worked in Leeds for a year and returned safely to Szeged he was then allowed to take his family on a short holiday to Austria. He never returned to Hungary and nobody was to blame except himself.

Joseph Imri was the first surgeon to come to Leeds. He knew no English at all, and when he arrived, in order not to inconvenience other people in the hospital who would perhaps address him in the meaningless language of English, he would always speak first and showing his English dictionary, say: 'Good morning, I am Dr. Imri from Hungary, I do not speak English'. Unfortunately for me one of the first people he encountered was the hospital secretary responsible for his salary. I was asked by the secretary why I had appointed a doctor to look after patients who could not speak a word of English. I replied that he would learn very soon, and of more importance was that he was a first class surgeon. Joseph Imri really was of outstanding ability. Just before he succeeded Professor Petri as Professor of Surgery to Szeged he died of an acute leukaemia, a tremendous loss to Hungary. He was one of the most talented young surgeons who ever worked with me.

In 1981 I was made a member of the Hungarian Surgical Society and in 1983 I was given the honorary degree of Doctor of Medicine at Szeged University.

15
The Fox That Foxed Me

During the war I was in Italy for over three years serving in a small mobile surgical unit. I visited almost every town and village starting at Reggio in Calabria and finishing in Cortina d'Ampezzo. I fell in love with the place.

After the war I returned at least once every year for I had made many friends with the same interests in surgery as myself. I was always invited to their meetings. On several occasions at the invitation of Professor Valdoni, I operated at the Policlinic in Rome.

He invited me to the wedding of his eldest daughter who married a prince, one of the Roman Grande Famiglia, and the festivities lasted a full week. It was a memorable and pleasant occasion. The one incident I remember to this day is that at the conclusion of the final banquet held immediately after the wedding ceremony, the bride and groom walked around their guests while they were still sitting at their tables, and presented everyone with a sugared almond on a small silver spoon engraved with their initials. I still have this spoon today.

Each winter in Leeds convinced me that it would be wonderful to own a property in Italy where I could go at any time of the year when I was free. I mentioned this thought to the Paliaga family in Rome stating that I was interested in the wilder underdeveloped Southern part of the country, possibly Calabria, rather than the richer North. Professor Aldo Paliaga drove me south in February, 1952. We went down the coast from Rome through Terracina, Sperlonga, Gaeta and then on to the outskirts of Naples but I was not impressed. Parts of Yorkshire were prettier. There were too many new developments taking place. Then Aldo told me he had read in the Italian magazines about a place called Capo Palinuro which had fantastic rock scenery and was exceedingly pretty. In fact, the rock scenery is some of the best in Europe and is why it was later chosen to film *Ulysses and the Golden Fleece*. Both Aldo and I wished to see the place so we drove on south through the most primitive and unspoilt country along mule tracks which locally were called roads. When we arrived in Palinuro it was dark, only one hotel was open. There was a welcoming fire in the sitting room. The eight hour journey from Rome had tired us, so after a meal we went to bed.

Next morning, we met the owner of the hotel who was enormously fat. He looked about the same size as his Porsche car which he proudly showed us. He offered to take us to a building site which was for sale but we were sure that he would fill the car himself, so we thanked him and told him that we had been driving the whole of yesterday and now preferred to have a walk. However, we watched him get into his car — a problem which he had mastered successfully. He would sit down backwards on the driving seat, then turn around bringing in his legs and finally he lifted his stomach into place pushing most of it behind and under the steering wheel. How he managed to manipulate all the controls was a mystery.

I walked with Aldo along a beach which was the best I had ever seen in Italy. It was quite unspoilt and like a garden with wild flowers such as sand holly, sand lilies and many more varieties of plants and flowers. It was really a paradise. I soon found a plot of land for sale bordering the beach which was ideal and just what I had been looking for. A farmer told us that we could meet the owner tomorrow, so we fixed a time at the site.

Returning to Palinuro we found that we were the only two guests at the hotel. However, the proprietor seemed to know some of our friends in Rome so in the evening he invited us to dine with him. Meanwhile, Aldo had been talking to some of the local people in the bar before dinner and he had made some interesting discoveries. The proprietor was a bachelor, but his frolics with the cook had produced sufficient personnel to cater for the hotel, so there was never any need to advertise for staff. The results had made it a sort of family affair.

At dinner the main course was fish, and seven were served in a dish swimming with olive oil. While I was dissecting my first one the proprietor ate at least three and he displayed an achievement which I had not seen before, and I would have thought impossible. While he continued to talk the fish bones were discharged at the angles of his mouth. He never coughed or choked and indeed never stopped talking. When he had finished the remainder of the fish he mopped up the oil with half loaves of bread which he ate. Aldo and I were glad when it was all over.

The next morning I met the owner of the plot of land we had found on the previous day. His nickname was the 'Fox' which I learned later was true to his character. He demonstrated the plot of land he wished to sell by meticulously inserting wooden pegs around its borders. It was not until a few years later I learned that the greater part of the land he sold to me was the beach, and did not belong to him at all, but to the local commune. Unfortunately, I trusted him and agreed to buy what he showed.

A month later I returned to complete the purchase and to sign various documents in the presence of my lawyer. Why at this time the lawyer didn't tell me I was buying the beach I do not know. When I arrived at his house, shouting could be heard in the street; there was a heated argument going on inside his office. The problem was that there was an olive tree growing on the dividing line between the land I was buying and the adjoining land. Both men were claiming ownership of the whole tree and were almost coming to blows about it. They quietened down when I suggested I would buy one half of the tree, and allow my neighbour to collect all the olives from it. This was no hardship to me, for Palinurian oil has a very strong taste and is far from pleasant to those who were not born there. An Italian from the village drew the first plan for me which looked quite ridiculous, a sort of bathing hut, in front of it were ducks swimming in the sea. I paid him but said nothing.

Returning home, I consulted an architect friend of mine called John Barrett. He volunteered to accompany me on the next visit to Palinuro which was in the summer of 1953. We studied the old farm buildings in the villages near to the land which I had bought. Most of them looked most attractive. John sketched some of these farms and we decided to build the house incorporating the features of these old buildings. The new plan was easily accepted by the Authority in Naples. The front terrace of the house faced the sea, having a roof supported by five arches and the whole structure was built of stone.

In 1953 there was no difficulty in finding experienced workmen because no developments were taking place so far south and there was keen competition for the work. A few years later this situation completely changed after the Italian Government commenced to pour money into the south in order to improve its standard of living. The result was that it ruined the countryside with cheap concrete buildings and did far more harm than good. My house was built entirely of stone, having walls approximately one metre thick. There were five arches covering the front terrace and open terraces at the sides of the house. The whole building looked excellent and it was considered to be the best in that area. One or two other houses later tried to copy the plan but they had not the same success. However, there was one serious fault made when it was built, and that was, the wooden framework of the windows had not been fitted correctly. They had not been recessed and protruded a little from the stone walls. This, unfortunately, allowed rain to come in when there was a north wind. During a storm, water would pour into the sitting room keeping everybody busy mopping it up with anything available. This happened when my first

The house in Italy — built on the beach.

John Moorman, Bishop of Ripon, on a visit.

English visitor arrived, John Moorman, Bishop of Ripon. He came to stay in February, 1955. One evening we experienced a violent storm and saw three water spouts following one another across the bay in front of the house, but they did not come inland and so we were safe. I would like to think that the Bishop's quotation from the Book of Job had some beneficial affect on abating the storm. He proved himself very useful in helping me to mop up the water in the sitting room. Eventually, Francesco Vanicore, my architect friend in Salerno, cured the defect of the windows satisfactorily by fitting louvres above them.

When the house was finally completed and furnished I gave a party to the local people, including two Mayors. One of the Mayors informed me that the house had been built on the beach, and so by Italian law belonged to him and not to me. Only the garden behind the house was mine. I didn't believe him, thinking that he was joking and dismissed his remarks. It was over a year later that I realised the seriousness of my situation. I received an ultimatum from the Capitano del Porto in Salerno saying that my house had been built entirely on the beach, it was a hazard to shipping, and had to be demolished. The loose stone of the building would belong to me, and he included a bill for carting it away to a quarry. The local commune had watched the foundations being dug and the building erected over a period of two years but said nothing until it was completed. I went to see my friends in Salerno and Rome asking if it were possible for me to buy the part of the beach on which the house had been built, but an old Italian law did not allow it. Eventually, I was granted a *commissioni*, under which I paid a ground rent to the commune for what was now leasehold property.

Aldo's father, Professor Attilio Paliaga, was physician to the Vatican and he told me that he was friendly with a lawyer in the housing department at the Government working in EUR, part of Rome. His job was to examine and deal with all the mistakes that people in Italy had committed unknowingly, similar to mine, and he thought it would be worth my while seeing him and obtaining his opinion. Ing Infante, the architect to the local Commune, Professor Bruno Paliaga, Aldo's brother, and myself went to see this lawyer at his office in EUR Rome. After passing many people in different corridors, all shouting and gesticulating, we eventually found the lawyer's office. Inside was impossible to believe. There were piles of documents at least four to five feet high covering every bit of the floor. I think without exaggeration there were certainly several thousand. Even the lawyer's desk was piled up with them so that he himself had only a narrow gap through which he could speak to us: and to make the situation more ridiculous still, the lawyer had a severe tic, so that every time he tried to talk to us, his face went into spasm. Bruno Paliaga whispered to me there was only one solution here, and that was to have a big fire. This visit to Rome achieved nothing except to reveal the disorganisation of one branch of their Government. The Capitano in Salerno continued to issue me with a commissioni each year provided I paid the ground rent, which increased yearly.

The house during its first two years of existence relied on bottle gas for light, supplying also a refrigerator and a cooker. There was no electricity. A well in the garden supplied water for the toilets and for washing but it was brackish and could not be drunk. Drinking water was obtained in bottles from the village. To supply the toilets, the well water was pumped into two large storage tanks in the false roof, and when they were full two ball valves closed to prevent them overflowing. When a central water supply eventually arrived to this area, the plumber connected the new water supply to the two storage tanks in the false roof but he didn't check to see whether the new system would work. The pressure of the central water supply proved to be too great for the ball valves to close, so the whole house was flooded.

Arriving from England one afternoon, before entering the house I saw water escaping from two vent holes at the side which allowed air to circulate in the false roof. Water was also pouring under the front door and down the front steps. Inside the house was chaos, there were at least six inches of water everywhere. The plaster on the walls had a crazy pattern and water was pouring out of every electric light switch. My bed and most of the furniture were soaked. I went to stay in an hotel, and it took at least six months for the house to dry out and be habitable again, but it recovered.

The next time the house was flooded, it was done intentionally. I let the place for the summer months in order to help to pay for the ground rent. The tenants were a bit untidy and when they left the floors were certainly very dirty, sand was everywhere from the beach. Luigi Fusco, a friend who owned an hotel in Palinuro, sent two of his char-ladies to clean the place for me. They took up all the carpets, removed their shoes and stockings, and then brought a hose pipe into the house flooding all the floors and getting rid of the sand satisfactorily. The legs of the furniture became accustomed to being drenched and did not appear to suffer unduly from their experience. I have a Georgian chest of drawers here in Leeds which survived all these insults and still presents a remarkably good patina.

The soil in the garden was of very poor quality so I bought a few loads of good top soil from a farm. The farmer brought it with his tractor and distributed it evenly over my garden. I didn't know until later that I had also bought one of the worst weeds in the world called arunda donax, which is mentioned in the old Testament, and I can believe that it may have been responsible for unsettling the Jews.

This weed in one season grows four to five feet high and sends out shoots at least fifteen feet long, which root again. So within one season it filled the whole of my garden. I brought a specimen of the weed back to England and showed it to Nigel Hepper, a half cousin who worked in the research department at Kew Gardens. He told me to spray with Round-Up, and within two years the weed had completely disappeared.

After the farmer's delivery of earth, we noticed that the kitchen sink and baths began to take a long time to empty but thought little of it at the time. Also, one of the oleander bushes in the centre of the garden grew at an alarming rate, outgrowing all the others. My nephews were staying at the house when the waste pipes and toilets became completely blocked. They called a plumber from the village who commenced to dig in the garden near to the rapidly growing oleander tree. He had not gone very far when black sewage as thick as oil sprang up into the air at least four to five feet. The smell was killing and quickly cleared the beach and surrounding countryside of all visitors. The main drains to the sump had been fractured by the farm tractor bringing the fresh soil for the garden. Fortunately, it was easily repaired.

One summer my sister, who had not yet seen the house in Palinuro, decided to take all her family there. I volunteered to carry her numerous requirements in my car and the family would follow later by air. My Austin Westminster, even without the rear seat, was absolutely full and there was only just sufficient room for me to drive. Everything went well until I was approaching Naples. At the end of the Autostrada, beyond the toll barrier, the road used to continue on for about a mile before joining an extremely busy road going to and from Naples. Approaching this busy road I discovered I had no brakes and as I was in overdrive top gear, there was no compression. Neither did the handbrake work. Pumping the footbrake achieved nothing. The car was only doing about thirty five miles an hour fortunately, but continued on towards the busy road, which was full of traffic. I was determined to stop it somehow before reaching this road. I steered it towards an iron post, but the post left its concrete base and the car went on. The only way of stopping the overloaded car now was to drive it towards a stone wall, which I did, but the impact, even at thirty five miles an hour, was much greater than I anticipated. I hit the steering wheel, cutting my lips and breaking my front teeth. The car looked a bit of a mess and so did I, but it could have been worse for both of us. While I was inspecting the damage to the car two workmen arrived with a large notice to fix on the post that I had just knocked down. When they saw it lying on the floor they roared with laughter and took the sign away. They had only erected the post the previous day. A nearby garage towed my car in and when they saw my coat covered with blood, offered me some whisky, which I declined. All I wanted was another vehicle to take the goods from the Austin to my house in Palinuro.

The garage had sold on hire purchase a new VW van to two youths who were finding it difficult to pay. The youths were summoned and agreed to take me the four hour journey to Palinuro. Their van was hardly large enough for the three of us and all the luggage and so some of it was strapped on to the roof rack. We reached the house about 2.30 am. I opened a few tins and made some sort of meal for them while they unpacked the van. Then we retired to bed. I could not sleep after such an exciting day. About half an hour later I heard the two youths in the sitting room where I had left my portfolio containing all my documents. I got up and saw both of them sorting out my papers. One youth explained that they were searching for a present from England while the other youth, who had a most unpleasant expression and looked a bad character, spoke in a broad Neapolitan accent which I couldn't understand. He was obviously planning something unpleasant. But the better looking of the two stopped him from talking any more. I thought the situation looked a bit ominous. The house is very isolated and cannot be seen from the road, I had no telephone and the port of Palinuro is about five miles away. I spoke to the more pleasant of the two youths, asking how much I owed them, and told him that they must leave immediately. Fortunately, they obeyed and my relief was never so great as when I locked the door behind them. The next morning I found that £200. in cash had been taken from my case, but my passport, traveller's cheques and cheque book were all there.

The Austin had been left at the garage where the two youths were well known, so I went to see the head of the Police in Salerno, who was a friend of mine, his wife being a former patient. I described what had happened and asked whether I should prosecute the two for stealing £200 but he advised me against it, saying they would almost certainly damage my house and perhaps burn it down if I tried to punish them, so I considered it prudent to do nothing. The damage to the car was not so great, although it looked much worse. Alfredo, a mechanic in Palinuro, went to see it. It required a new radiator which he fitted from another car but he was not able to repair the brakes. He and the custodian of my house drove the hundred miles from Naples to Palinuro without any brakes. This was over mountainous country roads, having something like two hundred bends, many of a hairpin character. How they managed it, I don't know but they did arrive safely and the car rested in an olive grove near my house in Palinuro for over a year until Appleyards in Leeds sent out the required parts. I was anxious not to leave the car in Italy as I wanted its registration number VUB 1 for another car, so I persuaded a motor mechanic in Palinuro to patch it up for me. I drove it back successfully to Leeds on my own the following year.

Every time I arrived in Palinuro I was besieged with people requesting medical or surgical advice. I was glad to help and received many kindnesses in return for I would never take any money from them. They were always exceedingly generous, bringing me crates of fresh fruits, vegetables, homemade cheeses, etc. One day I was presented with some live hens which we put in the garage. Andrew, my nephew, was staying with me at the time and remarked when the hens arrived: 'Uncle Geoff, please don't see any more patients otherwise we shall never get into the house'.

One day a young man in uniform came to consult me. He looked like a soldier but he proved to be a guardian of the forests. He had seen the local doctor who said he had colitis and gave him some medicine, but the pain in his abdomen had become worse and he really felt very ill. I examined him and decided he had an acute gall bladder, which should be removed as soon as possible. I spoke to my friend the surgeon at the hospital in Agropoli, who agreed to admit him immediately and remove his gall bladder. When the young man left my house he forgot his cap; and just as he was leaving my drive to enter his car which was parked on the road, a cavalcade of cars arrived from

Naples. A Professor Agostini was in the first car, he also had the rank of General and was accompanied by a Lieutenant, while the retinue followed in cars behind. The General never liked the young man whom I had just examined, and to see him without his cap was infuriating. The young man explained that he had just been examined by an English Professor of Surgery. The General disbelieved him saying, 'No English Professor could possibly live in such an isolated place'. I was in my house while this discussion was taking place, not knowing what was happening until the door bell rang. The Lieutenant speaking a little English said to me 'Good morning, the General does not believe that you are a Professor' to which I answered 'Good morning, tell him that I do not think he is a General' which had a dramatic effect. The General came to greet me, embraced me and we became the best of friends. He soon found out that I was interested in flowers and gardening, so every time I visited Italy subsequently he would come to see me bringing conifers and shrubs to plant in the garden and he helped me himself to do it. One day he showed me where the Primula Palinuro grows and I took two of these rare plants to Kew as well as a rare fern which is scented and only grows in laval dust on Vesuvius. We had many happy times together until he retired and returned to his native Trieste.

A small stream bordered the north side of my garden dividing it from a field on the other side which I also owned. The fresh water in the stream from the hills attracted snakes and on four occasions I was spat at by vipers in my own garden but I never saw them. They were always hidden in the tall grass. I was advised always to wear rubber boots until the grass had been cut.

One summer Andrew, my nephew, and Laura Valdoni and Sylvia Villoresi from Rome were staying with me. My nephew told me that he had seen about four small grey coloured snakes come from under the front terrace towards the beach. The following day Laura Valdoni told me that she had seen a much larger black snake climbing up the garage wall. So far they hadn't disturbed us and, we were told that black snakes were good at catching mice and rats, so we didn't interfere with them. However, one night we were all awakened about 2.00 am by a banging noise in the false roof above our bedrooms. The noise was so great that we thought the ceilings might collapse. It continued for about half an hour and then all was quiet. Next morning we consulted our custodian who was convinced it was a black rat snake killing the mice or rats in the false roof. Later we saw one of the adults which was more than six feet long making its way across the beach to its abode underneath the front terrace where Andrew had previously seen the small grey ones. This perturbed us a little and we thought we would ask advice from some of the local people. The nearest building to my house was a taverna and I went to speak to the owner. He thought we should try and kill the adult snakes. He offered to call a girl from Palinuro who was a snake charmer and considered the best time to catch them would be the late afternoon or early evening. So, about 6.00 o'clock the next day two waiters from the taverna, the snake charmer, my custodian, and ourselves all duly armed, gathered on the front terrace. The snake charmer started to make a sort of wailing noise which reminded me of a Mullah in Cairo calling everybody to prayer. She carried on intermitently for almost an hour but nothing appeared. The party was becoming a failure so to cheer them up I brought out some red wine and my tape recorder on which I played Bert Kamphert's 'Dancing Safari'. It had been playing for only a short time when we saw a large black snake advancing on the sands towards us. The excitement was terrific. Everyone started to arm themselves with sticks, stones etc. As it approached the terrace, my custodian hit it on the head with a large stone, stunning it. The two waiters from the taverna jumped down from the terrace on to the sands and finished it off, then they dragged it across the sands to the sea. It measured over six feet long but the surprising thing was that the next morning it had gone and I never knew how this had happened. Perhaps dogs had taken it away. We then lit a fire near to the snakes' abode under the terrace, burning old rubber tyres which had the desired effect for we never saw any more black snakes that year. But next year the persistent creatures returned in force to the same abode, and we decided to ignore them.

For many years the Italian workmen never appear to be satisfied with their pay. One Union or another calls for a one-day strike, which beforehand is published in the Press so you are always warned what to expect. Before such warnings were announced, I was travelling by train from Naples to Rome when the train stopped half way at Cassino. We saw the engine driver and his mate leave the train and walk away carrying their belongings. At first, we thought they were changing drivers, but when after about half an hour no replacement returned, we became a little restive. Then somebody appeared going from carriage to carriage asking if there was anyone present who could drive the train. We watched outside the window to see if anybody volunteered. Eventually, a youth in his late teens said he knew what to do, and the passengers appeared to believe him. He took over and drove the train the remaining sixty miles to Rome at no more than thirty miles an hour, but we did arrive safely.

Another occasion, I was on an Alitalia flight going to Rome when I discovered the cabin stewards were on strike. After speaking to the two pilots they allowed me to serve the meals and drinks. There were only sixteen of us in the Caravelle but we finished the supplies of champagne without charge. It was one of the best flights I have ever had.

On another occasion, I had driven from Yorkshire to Rome in my car and retired to bed early because I was tired. The next morning I was told that there had been a severe earthquake in the Salerno region where I was going. I didn't realise how bad it was until I arrived there. The town was deserted and it reminded me of my first visit during the war. I had an appointment to see my lawyer in the evening, so after passing down deserted streets and seeing two blocks of flats completely demolished, I booked a room at the Plaza Hotel which looked intact. I dined with my lawyer, who left immediately afterwards in his car for the country, and then I returned to the hotel to sleep. About 2.00 am I hit the wall next to my bed or the wall hit me. It was an after-shock and only lasted a few moments but I don't think it caused any further damage to the town.

Next morning I set off early in the Austin for my house in Palinuro which is a four hour drive. Practically all the way both sides of the road were parked cars, packed together with their owners and families sleeping inside. When I arrived in Palinuro I found the house was occupied by my friend, Francesco Vanacore, and his family. He informed me that because my house was built on sand it was relatively safe from earth tremors, a comforting thought because I could never persuade any insurance company to cover it for storm or damage by earthquakes.

Two evenings later I was on my own reading when a crack appeared in the floor where I was sitting, my chair descended about two inches. The sitting room was the only room with a cellar under it so I went to bed, feeling safer in my own bedroom. The next morning an inspection revealed that the sitting room floor had no beams or girders to support it, but was made only of concrete reinforced with wire netting. How it had managed to stay up was a mystery. It was obvious that the whole of the floor had to be renewed, which was no small undertaking. I thought this was a legitimate excuse to renew all the domestic appliances in the house which I had brought originally from England. It was quite impossible to buy spare parts which from time to time were required; they were unobtainable in Italy. It took several weeks for the alterations to be accomplished. As well as replacing the kitchen and bathroom equipment, I installed a central heating system. Later, while in England, I was informed that everything was finished and that it was all in perfect order. I drove over one January to enjoy the comfort of the house with the central heating working. The plumber, proud of his work, escorted me around wishing to show me what he had done before he asked for payment. But first I had to go to the toilet, having driven for four hours. When I pulled the string to flush the basin it was flushed with almost boiling water. Hot water came out of cold taps and cold water out of the hot ones. It was really more amusing than serious and was quickly corrected.

Whilst I was staying there at this time in January I noticed that uniformed policeman were parading up and down the beach in the evenings in front of my house and also on the road behind it. One evening I enquiried what it was all about, and it appeared that the two miles of sandy beach in front of my house was ideal for small craft to come over from North Africa carrying drugs. They had already caught three. I felt secure with the police guarding the beach at night until the Mayor came to speak to me one evening. He asked if I was in the house on my own, whether I had a pistol and said I should certainly get one if I intended to stay for long. It transpired that somebody had been kidnapped from the village next to Palinuro and the demand was equivalent to about £500,000 sterling for his release. I knew my house was only about forty miles away from where Paul Getty's son had been held but until now I had not really been unduly worried about it. I was certainly not a millionaire but the Mayor's visit did disturb me a little. When I returned to England, my brother, who was a solicitor, wanted to insure me against being kidnapped but I told him that this might encourage somebody to ask for more, if it happened.

Before starting to build the house I had obtained permission from the Bank of England to send to Italy approximately £20,000 in American dollars. This transfer of currency had a 30% premium.

I dispatched about £1,000 at a time when requested. The money always left England immediately but it would be held up by the Italian Bank for at least a month before it was released in lire.

An acquaintance of mine in Palinuro agreed to obtain the lire from the local bank and pay the workmen for me. One day his wife telephoned me asking me to send some more money quickly otherwise the builders would stop working. One of my colleagues in Leeds was going on holiday to Palinuro and offered to take £500 in cash, to satisfy the workmen while I arranged to send another £1,000 through the bank.

About two years later I discovered that this so called 'friendly' acquaintance in Palinuro had managed to transfer about half of my land into his name, excusing himself by saying that he wished to develop it for me, and any development must be done in an Italian's name.

My friends in Rome told me that this was not true. He refused to listen to reason and return the land to me so I consulted my lawyer, who wrangled with him for about a year and then advised me to prosecute him.

I engaged two barristers. The first was born near Palinuro, an enormous man with an aggressive face which would frighten a bull, a great advantage if you are a criminal lawyer. Hair came out of every orifice and his voice drowned the courtroom even when everybody seemed to be shouting at one another. At the trial he kept reinforcing himself with ramazzotti which he had stored in a corner, but his voice certainly had no need of reinforcement. I noticed that when he was shouting, my friends from Rome put their fingers to their ears and told me that his language was worse than anything in the Navy.

The other barrister was advisor to our embassy in Rome. He was of a gentle character, less than five feet high, and only people near to him could hear what he was saying.

I remember sitting down on a chair and saying to my friends from Rome, 'I do not know what it is costing but it is damn funny'.

The trial was really a shouting match between the different lawyers. No decision was made, but a retrial six months later decided in my favour.

Before my lawyers had issued the first summons to the acquaintance who had stolen my land, he tried to blackmail me, saying that if I continued with the prosecution he would inform my bank that I had sent £500 illegally without paying the dollar premium. I immediately went and told my bank manager about it in Leeds, saying I would rather go to prison in England than be blackmailed in Italy. My bank manager took me to the Queen's Hotel in Leeds and treated me to a champagne lunch. I told him that it appears you have to be a naughty boy before the bank will provide you with a free champagne lunch. I paid the dollar premium on the £500, and nothing more happened.

Later on, I discovered that you could legally send goods abroad, sell them, and so obtain foreign currency to avoid paying the high dollar premium. I bought a considerable amount of second hand furniture from the salerooms in and around Leeds, sufficient to fill a large pantechnicon. Turnbulls of Leeds, the carriers, wrapped each article in waterproof paper and the whole consignment arrived safely in Rome. Professor Valdoni allowed me a room in his house for storing the furniture but this was soon filled to capacity. We then filled his basement and finally, his garage. There was a mountain of paper in his garden after the unpacking had been finished by my friend Sylvia Villoresi. She was in charge of selling the furniture. Everything sold easily except three marble clocks which nobody would buy, they were ugly, and too heavy for any normal person to lift. We made little profit on the consignment but at least I had acquired some Italian lire legally without having to pay the high dollar premium. When I returned to Rome three months later I collected the remaining marble clocks, put them into the boot of my car and tried to sell them to the small antique shops in the centre of the city, but without success. I was soon tired of lifting them in and out of the car. I remembered one small shop near the island of

Tiberina which belonged to an elderly gentleman. I went to see him and carried the three into his shop, putting them on the counter. He too didn't appear to be interested and wouldn't buy them. I was determined not to carry them anymore, so I told him he could have the lot as a present. I then left as fast as possible, because I was sure he could not lift them himself without assistance.

In the next chapter on Yugoslavia, I describe my meeting with the Grieve family from Scotland, and recall how Simon, the husband, was taken acutely ill while staying with me in Korcula, and died in Dubrovnik Hospital. The following summer I invited Helen, his widow, and Fiona, their daughter, to stay with me in Palinuro.

At this time Fiona was working at our Embassy in Rome. She spoke fluent Italian and knew most of the dialects. In my garage there was an old Fiat car belonging to my nephew, Andrew Hepper, which anybody could use while staying there. It was neither licensed nor insured. Helen and Fiona decided to take the Fiat to Palinuro and do some shopping while I amused myself in the garden.

While they were going up my drive to reach the main road the whole exhaust fell off producing a deafening noise. I told them to drive slowly and not to worry as everybody in Palinuro, including the Police, knew the car well, because it had been there for over six years. Unfortunately, on this particular Saturday morning, a Colonel from the Salerno Police and his Lieutenant were there to check the activities of the local Police, when my car approached making a thunderous noise. They stopped it, and Fiona in Palinuron dialect said something to them which was supposed to be funny but the Colonel thought otherwise. This resulted in both ladies being arrested and questioned. I was waiting in the house for their return which seemed a long time. When they appeared, they were both under arrest, and escorted by two Police Officers. I telephoned my custodian, and asked him to come and help us immediately. He arrived unshaven and looking very untidy. I explained the situation to him. He began to look really angry and went up to the Police Officers with hands in his trouser pockets, and more or less shouted in their faces something I couldn't understand. When I asked Fiona she had difficulty in translating it, but what it really amounted to was 'b----- off'. The Officers didn't move and I visualised all of us going to prison. Then the custodian walked a few paces nearer to the Police and, in a much louder voice, shouted again 'b----- off'. There was a moment's deadly silence, then the Officers saluted me and walked away. We retired to the house, and Fiona told me that only the Mafia could behave like this. The custodian had been in my employment for over fifteen years. I had never suspected him of belonging to any secret organisation, but I had thought that he had some inside knowledge of what was happening locally when, on two or more occasions, I found him sleeping in my garage which he said was a precaution to prevent myself or my nephew being molested.

The authorities in Salerno still refused to allow me to buy the land on which the house was built, and every year my ground rent increased. I was allowed only to sell the garden as the house belonged to the Maritime Authority on whose land it stood, but I could sell the 'commissioni' which would allow the next owner the tenancy of the house.

Finally, when at last I decided to sell the house, I took my godson, Ted Milostic, with me to help to pack some of the antique furniture which would be highly suitable for a barn I was converting into a house at West Burton in the Yorkshire Dales. One pleasant evening, Ted suggested dining outside in the garden under the pine trees. It was dark when we commenced the meal but the lights from a nearby terrace provided us with sufficient light to see what we were about to enjoy. Just as we had sat down, before we commenced to eat, Ted asked me to look up at the trees. There were rows and rows of glistening eyes looking down in our direction from well over a hundred brown rats, wondering how much we would leave. I dislike people watching me when I am eating, it always puts me off my food. This time was the largest audience I have ever had, but not for long; we quickly carried our meal into the house and decided that the kitchen table was more attractive than pine trees.

I was extremely fond of the property but as I grew older it became more difficult for me to visit. The journey by car is three days from Yorkshire. The flights were via Naples, a quite impossible place, the congestion around the airport is still the worst in Europe.

I informed two of my closest friends, Francesco Infante and Luigi Fusco, that I had decided to sell the property. I did not wish to make another mistake selling, as I had when I bought the land. They advised me to keep quiet about it, and they would enquire from people whom they could trust, which in that area are scarce.

But the news spread to more sinister quarters when furniture was seen being taken out of the house. I had some really terrifying people to see me, wishing, or so they said, to buy. One had the worst face I have ever seen on any human being, it was like the ones you see on the paintings of hell and purgatory. He was very persistent and came at night three times: fortunately I was never alone in the house.

I had Lady Jean Carr and Mrs. Joanna Lucas staying with me. They were of great help in a difficult situation, nothing frightened them. I discovered too that they were experts at clearing a house. Everything portable, and considered

Evacuating Palinuro: (above) lunching with Joanna Lucas; (below) Lady Jean Carr so exhuasted she had to be fed.

perhaps not necessary, they carried on to the beach for me to burn. But I am a hoarder and objects which I had not seen for twenty years appeared. So while they were busy on step ladders emptying the cupboards, I was just as busy carrying things back into the house, storing them in my bedroom for safety.

What surprised me and upset me the most was when my custodian, whom I had befriended and employed for more than twenty years, demanded a large sum of money from me. The whole situation had turned sour. I was glad therefore when a friend of both Francesco and Luigi offered me a reasonable amount in American dollars which I accepted. The sale was completed in August, 1991 — perhaps I should have taken the architect, John Barrett's, advice back in 1963 when he said to me, 'My advice to you is to get rid of it now because the people are too clever for you'.

16

Pig in a Suitcase

In 1951 a Yugoslav surgeon visited the Leeds Infirmary. He particularly wished to see the work which we were doing in the Department of Thoracic Surgery. He introduced himself as Professor Lavric of Ljubljana University, and so that I could keep in touch with him he gave me the address of the hotel where he was staying. I knew this hotel well and its reputation. It was small, most unpleasant and catered almost entirely for young students at the University. I invited him to stay with me at my house in Clarendon Road, and he gladly accepted. I found him to be an extremely pleasant person and we quickly became great friends. I persuaded him to stay with me for as long as he could; after obtaining permission from his Government he was allowed to remain for almost three weeks. Six months later he returned to Leeds for a short visit in order to persuade me to visit his surgical unit in Ljubljana, so the following summer of 1953 I went over by train to see him. I discovered when I arrived there that Professor Lavric was a great friend of Marshal Tito. He had just successfully operated on him, removing a large stone from his common bile duct which had been missed when his gall bladder was removed in Belgrade.

The University Hospital at Ljubljana was not a military hospital so received little financial help from the Government. They were short of hard currency and were unable to buy expensive surgical equipment from abroad, but this did not dismay them and with the help of the Engineering Department of the University they built their own heart/lung machine. Most of this work was achieved by a young surgeon called Miro Kosac who later succeeded Professor Lavric as Professor of Surgery. I saw this machine working successfully in their experimental operating theatre, where they were operating on dogs. I was most impressed with their work. I gave one or two lectures about the oesophagus and lungs and closed heart surgery. Then Professor Lavric suggested that I should go to speak at the University of Sarajevo where his friend was Professor of Surgery. The most convenient way of going there was to take the train from Zagreb, it being about two hours by road from Ljubljana. I decided to spend two days in Zagreb on the way with my friends, the Dominkovic family, whose son was a Doctor of Medicine and had worked in Leeds.

Late one afternoon a driver with a Jeep called on me at the Slon Hotel in Ljubljana. With the help of an interpreter he asked whether I wished to go on an interesting mountainous route to Zagreb or to take the main road. I chose the mountainous route. The driver was an unusual character, he was wearing shorts, an open neck shirt and appeared to be covered all over with long hair, but he was very competent at his job. After we had covered about half the journey along a dusty track, he stopped at a building in a small primitive looking village. We entered a very large room which had a fire in the centre of the earthen floor. A hole in the ceiling allowed some of the smoke to escape, preventing us from being suffocated. Several whole beasts had been roasted on long poles and they were hung up on the wall behind the fire, so I was offered a choice of roast pig, goat, lamb etc. I chose lamb and red wine. A full litre was brought to each of us. The meat was excellent but the wine impossible. I tasted it and demonstrated I couldn't drink it so the driver finished both bottles. It didn't affect his driving, and we arrived quite safely in Zagreb. I spent a restful two days with Marko Dominkovic and his wife. In the evening of the third day Marko took me to the railway station and put me on the night train to Sarajevo arriving early next morning. A young surgeon from Sarajevo University met me at the station and escorted me to the Europa Hotel in the centre of the town. After breakfast, I was walking around the old city when a Moslem funeral procession approached me. There were about fifty mourners walking in a file, four abreast, behind the coffin. Being interested to know what their service was like I joined on to the rear of the column and followed them into a Mosque, but it was not for long. Two men escorted me outside when I refused to remove my only pair of shoes.

I was not impressed with the hospital at Sarajevo, and decided to leave the following evening on the night train for Dubrovnik which departed just before midnight. After booking a seat on the train I was wondering how I could fill up the time before the train left. The hotel receptionist suggested the opera, but when I went to the box office at the Opera House I was told that all seats had been sold. A soldier standing near to me understood my poor German and offered to sell me his friend's ticket because his friend was on guard duty that evening and couldn't attend. It cost me a shilling (5p). After dinner, I returned to the Opera House and found myself in the orchestra stalls in the midst of the Yugoslav army, sitting next to the soldier who had sold me his friend's ticket. I appeared to be the only one there in mufti which created a certain amount of attention, and more than a few not understandable remarks. After the opera the same soldier accompanied me to the Hotel Europa and being short of time we hurriedly collected my suitcase and then he escorted me safely to the train for Dubrovnik, which left about midnight. I shared a second class compartment with two portly gentlemen sitting opposite me, and an attractive young mother with two children on my side. She fortunately spoke good French so I was able to communicate with her. When I had bought my ticket in Sarajevo I had been informed that there was a buffet bar attached to the train, but this proved to be untrue. We had been travelling for about an hour when I enquired about the buffet, remarking that I was rather hungry. The message was passed on in Serbo-Croat to the two portly gentlemen, and one of them reached for his suitcase in the luggage rack. When he opened it, it appeared to contain no clothes and the first thing that we saw was a whole pig already roasted, and bottles of slivovic, onions and brown bread. He divided the pig with a hunting knife and we were all given liberal portions. The only implement I had with me was a large nail file, but it functioned successfully both as a fork and table knife. After this most welcome meal one of the gentleman started to sing Dalmatian songs and I responded by singing *On Ilkley Moor baht 'at.* Then, in order to aid digestion, we started to dance up and down the corridor but, being very tired, this did not last long, and we settled down for the night, each having a corner seat. The peace did not last long: an extremely loud knocking noise started under our floorboards and then the boards commenced to move upwards, which convinced us that there was a serious problem and possibly something heavy would break through. We all put our feet and legs up on the seats in order to obtain some degree of protection, but the noise alerted the guard, because after a few minutes of violent banging the train stopped and everybody got outside. We were in a wild and desolate part of the country and all I could see were cactus plants of the prickly pear variety. I remember asking the mother of the two children whether it was North Africa. I had a pocket torch with me, so I went under our carriage to inspect what had happened. A large piece of metal attached to the brakes had become loose and was causing the trouble. It was not possible to repair it, so we were told to leave our carriage which was shunted into a siding. All the other carriages of the train were just open cattle trucks, ours having been the only one with a roof and padded seats. The occupants of the trucks were all standing because there was not sufficient room to sit down. However, I soon discovered that being cramped together like sardines in a vertical position did keep your body warm, only your head suffered. At about five o'clock in the morning we reached Mostar. While we were having coffee at the station cafe another second class carriage was coupled on to the rear of the train and we were conducted to it. We had the great luxury of a roof and padded seats again. My companions and myself, all having suffered equally, became quite friendly, but we decided not to talk any more but try to sleep. About half an hour out of Mostar the train stopped: two Yugoslav soldiers with red stars on their caps entered our compartment and asked for identity cards or passports. I searched through my pockets and suitcase but couldn't find my passport and then I remembered that in a hurry to catch the train I had left it in the Hotel Europa at Sarajevo. With the help of the young mother to interpret for me I explained what had happened. The soldier appeared not to believe me and said that I must identify myself. I showed him my Barclays travellers cheques, issued in Leeds, the shirt I was wearing had a Matthias Robinson, Leeds, label: finally I showed him my vaccination marks but the soldier was not amused and ordered me to go to the guard room if I had no identity papers. Then I remembered the letter from Professor Lavric inviting me to Ljubljana which I had in a separate compartment of my suitcase. After the soldier had read this letter from Tito's friend and surgeon, he sprang to attention and for the first time speaking in Italian asked if I really was a friend of Professor Lavric. Then he left the train, and called out the guard which formed up outside my carriage window. As I was wearing only an open-neck shirt and shorts I quickly put on my jacket. They all saluted me and I shook every one of them by the hand. I told them that I was going to stay at the Excelsior Hotel in Dubrovnik. They promised me that my passport would arrive there the following afternoon, which indeed it did.

The sequel to this passport episode was that next year I was invited to lunch with the Yugoslav Ambassador in London while Professor Lavric was staying with him. I told this story to the Ambassador and looking at Professor Lavric I said, 'You know you have a funny country, your letter seems to be of more importance than my passport'. The Ambassador didn't look amused so I changed the subject quickly.

I had a wonderful few days in Dubrovnik. Everybody was so friendly. The first day I was there I went down to the beach to swim. Dressed in my swimming trunks I created a considerable amount of attention because my skin was absolutely white and I was also rather thin. Some youngsters ventured near asking if I were German. I do not think they had seen an Englishman before, because they looked so surprised when I said I had come from England. They went to their homes and returned with their English lesson books, so each morning I gave them a lesson on the sands. It was great fun, I was invited to their homes and one evening they took me to an excellent concert. It was a most enjoyable few days; I was determined to return when I had the chance. I had acquired an affection for this country which has remained with me all my life.

About eighteen months later Professor Lavric started to have difficulty with his speech and a weakness was noticed on the right side of his body. He came over to St. Mary's Hospital in London and his left internal carotid artery was decoked. He returned to Ljubljana but continued to deteriorate, losing his speech almost completely. I was requested to see him because an x-ray of his chest showed shadows in both lungs. The doctors were wondering whether he could have a lung cancer and a secondary in his brain. Marshall Tito had lent him his villa on Lake Bled, and after arriving at Ljubljana airport I was taken there by car to see him. After examining him and seeing his x-rays I was convinced there was no cancer. He was in an extremely weak state, and had not the strength to swallow properly. The shadows in his lungs were due to inhaling food and fluid. I spent two days with him trying to cheer him up but he could not talk to me and most of the time was crying. He was a gentleman, an excellent surgeon and as I had become very fond of him, it was most depressing to see him in this condition. I was really distressed to learn that he died soon after I had left him.

I was invited by two doctors to go for a short holiday on the island of Korcula. One of the doctors was Tomica Dominkovic, whom I have mentioned before. His family had lived in the old city of Korcula for a hundred years and they possessed at least three houses. We took the ship from Rijeka in Northern

Korcula, Croatia.

Croatia to Korcula which arrived at about two o'clock in the morning. We followed Tomica up a completely dark passageway and climbed the most irregular steps I have ever encountered. At the top of the steps, Tomica called to his aunt and she opened the door of her house for us, which I think had not changed very much since the 16th Century. We were led up to the second floor under a low roof. You could stand up only in the middle of the room, so it was advisable to sleep facing the outer wall otherwise when you sat up in bed you hit your head on the rafters. The morning following our arrival we went to the Planjak restaurant to meet the fourth member of our party. He was Jura Valentekovic, who arrived in uniform for he had been discharged from his period of military service only that morning. We spent five happy days fishing around the hundreds of small islands which surround the main island. Every day brought success, and after making a fire on one of the islands we would grill the fish, which tasted delicious. I am afraid I did little else but sit in the boat, swim and help to eat the fish. This life was a completely new experience for me. I had never before received such warm hospitality, and Korcula's magnificent Venetian architecture created the most beautiful town I had seen. The whole place enchanted me, so next year I returned to ask if it were possible to buy one of the old houses and restore it. Yugoslavia, being a Communist state, did not allow foreigners to buy property. I made enquiries with my friends about my position and I was told by a lawyer in Korcula that if I could find a reliable Yugoslav, and put the property into his or her name, then legally it could pass to me when they died. Not being anxious for any of my friends to die quickly, I was rather nervous of asking someone to do this for me, but Tomica's aunt, Linka Dominkovic, gladly accepted the responsibility. I chose a ruin near to the cathedral which had only three walls, no floors, no roof and a tree growing in the middle of what remained of the building. But the magnificent stonework of the beautiful facade with its balcony was one of the most attractive in Korcula.

I bought it from the Donadini family, who originally came from Venice. In all probability, it was quite a simple building before they rebuilt it during the 17th century, creating something in the best Venetian style. One remaining member of his family, living in Rijeka, came to see the house and congratulated me on what I had achieved, but I deserved no praise, it was owed to Linka's husband, Sime Dominkovic, who organised and carried out all the restoration work. I think it is true to say that this was the first ruined house in the city to be restored. Sir Fitzroy and Lady MacLean quickly followed the example with a house at the other side of the Piazza to mine.

Sime had a difficult task; the narrow street leading from the quayside has forty six steps to the entrance of the house so a sort of temporary railway was

The early 17th century façade of the house in Korcula.

With (left to right) Tomica Dominkovic with his Uncle Sime Dominkovic who organised and renovated the Korcula house so perfectly.

constructed of wood on which the wagons carrying building material could be pulled up by hand. Provided there was sufficient manpower, it was an ideal way of dealing with the situation. I asked Sime to restore the house as near as possible to its original state, retaining all the carved 16th and 17th century stonework which is so very attractive. But he had difficulty in placing the three floors. The original corbels were intact but to use them would have meant that no normal person could stand up straight, so the floors had to be adjusted to allow sufficient headroom for 20th century humanity.

When I first went to Korcula about a third of the old houses in the City appeared to be in ruins. Some had not been repaired since they were burnt down in the 16th Century to prevent spread of the plague. Others were damaged more recently during the second World War. But the city is beautiful, an artist's paradise, and today nearly all the old houses have been repaired and are lived in.

While the repairs were progressing, I was able to visualise the architectural plan of the old city because it interested me. It had been built on a small circular hill — at the summit is the cathedral, and from this central position the streets radiate down to the sea like the spokes of a wheel.

Only the fronts of the old houses have windows facing the narrow streets. The rear of the houses in one street are separated by a gap about one metre wide from the backs of the houses in the adjoining street.

Before a proper drainage system was introduced recently, these gaps at the rear of the houses, radiating down to the sea, acted as open drains, and everything conveniently disappeared into the porous rock on which the city is built. This ingenious method worked well until this century, and caused considerable interest to my architect friends. There were no drains to become blocked. The 'loos' were built on the rear walls of the houses discharging directly into the gap through a hole in the wall.

All the old houses collected rain water from the roofs, storing it in cisterns built in the basements of the houses. It was all right for washing and cooking, but unpleasant to drink. Bottled water came from the mainland which cost more than the local wine, but now there is an excellent water supply from the mountains in central Croatia.

Originally a thin strip of land connected the hill on which Korcula was built to the main island (also called Korcula). This strip of land was dug away during early times so that the city became surrounded by sea, and with a high curtain

Everything in Korcula is fascinating. With (from left to right) Prof Harry Schumacker, Mrs Myrtle Schumacker, Joanna Lucas and Bruno Paliaga with Marco Polo's house in the background.

wall it presented a formidable position to attack. The Greeks named the island Kokyria Melana (Korcula the Black) because it was covered with tall pine trees, giving it a dark appearance. In fact, the whole of the Dalmation coast used to be thickly wooded, until the Ventians removed the tall pine trees, using them as piles on which they built their houses and palaces.

Marco Polo is supposed to have lived in Korcula and a house bearing his name is only a few yards from my own.

During the Napoleonic wars, when the island was occupied by the British Navy, a Captain Lowen was in charge of the city. He built a gun emplacement of stone to guard the straits between Korcula and the mainland. The object was to stop Napoleon supplying his army in Egypt. The gun emplacement is still there today, and is known as the English Tower.

The English Tower, built by the Royal Navy in 1813 on a hill overlooking Korcula, is a gun emplacement to stop Napoleon supplying his army in Egypt.

Capt. Lowen also built a large semi-circular bench in carved stone where people can sit and admire the view towards the Pelejac peninsula. Unfortunately, the view is now largely obscured by trees. His name is carved on a stone pillar at the entrance.

But the British sailors were not always as friendly and well behaved as we should like to imagine. One of my friends, Mr. Joso Fazinic, while examining some of the old manuscripts and records of the city, came across an account written in Italian during the British occupation.

The document states that two of our sailors rowed over to Orebic on the mainland where they saw a young farmer with a pig, which they demanded from him: because he would not part with his pig, they shot him, threw his body into the

Captain Peter Lowen, RN, showed his appreciation of the people of Korcula when he left in 1815 by providing them with a place where they could sit and enjoy a view across to the mainland.

sea and took the pig. After our sailors had left, the local inhabitants retrieved the body and buried him in the churchyard.

It took over two years to restore my house properly. When the repairs were finished I sent most of the furniture from England in two large wooden crates. They were too heavy to lift off the ship when they arrived, so were unpacked on deck and then had to be carried up the forty six steps to the house, because Sime's wooden railway had been dismantled. A chest of drawers and two cabinets were too large for the staircase in the house so windows were removed to the first and second floors and the pieces hauled up outside with a winch.

After the crates had been unpacked on the ship, Sime made use of the timber by putting a floor in the false roof of the house which still has 'Turnbulls Leeds' painted on it.

Finally the house was furnished, clean and ready for occupation. As is the custom in Korcula I asked the priest, Father Ivo Matijaca, to come and bless it for me. He arrived one morning in his white cassock carrying a jug of holy water from the cathedral. He climbed up the stairs to the top of the house and the first room to be blessed and sprinkled with holy water was the toilet — it has never failed me.

One day after lunching with my dear friend, Capt. Balarin, I met a neighbour called Mr. Petkovic who was waiting at the bus stop with a suitcase near his

Plaque at entrance to house with Latin verse composed by the Professor of Latin at the Vatican, and presented to Geoffrey Wooler by Dr Attilio Paliaga. Translated it reads :
'To himself and his friends
This house
(disgraced by the wrongs of time
and the age of the structure)
Geoffrey Wooler
English doctor of wounds
Lover and supporter of Venetian art
To its ancient form of noble grace
He took care of its restoration
Year 1964.

feet. He greeted me in broken German: I thought he was asking for help with his luggage because he lived opposite me and had many steps to climb. The suitcase was the heaviest I have ever lifted, but together both holding on to the handle we were able to manage. When we arrived at his house he refused to allow it in, saying 'Nein, nein, nein'. He insisted on taking it to my house, and carried it there himself, leaving it on my doorstep. I was inquisitive to know what it contained, it certainly was not clothing, it was much too heavy. So I opened it, and underneath a well-used pullover there were hundreds of coins mostly of silver and copper. I really did not know what to do, and wondered if they had been stolen, and he wished me to take them back to England to sell them, because he knew I was leaving the following day. Then I thought of going to the police, but this might be a mistake, involving Petkovic and myself in a criminal investigation. The coins were obviously worth a lot of money, but who did they belong to and why did Petkovic insist that I should accept them? I could not understand his German sufficiently for him to explain. My father always told me, when in doubt wait. So I opened a bottle of wine and sat down for about half an hour contemplating what to do next. Mr. and Mrs. Peter Irving from London have a house in Korcula and they were staying there on holiday. I went to see them and told them that I had a hoard of treasure in my house which did not belong to me and what was I to do with it?

They both walked back to my house with me, and we had not been there long before the whole saga began to unravel.

Don Ivo, the high priest of Korcula, wished to transfer the collection of coins from his museum to one in Zagreb. His brother had agreed to take them, but he found that the collection was so large he could carry only one half of it at a time. He had taken the first half to the bus stop and asked Petkovic to look after it while he fetched the second half. When he returned to the bus stop with the second half and found that both Petkovic and the suitcase were missing he burst into tears, then rushed to tell his brother. They mobilised his whole family to find out who had stolen them.

Fortunately, one of the family had seen Petkovic and myself struggling to carry away the first suitcase, and very soon it was safely restored to Don Ivo's brother in time for him to catch the bus to Zagreb.

One autumn, Sime Dominkovic and his wife, Linka, went to stay with their relations in Rijeka. While they were there Sime became ill, complaining of no appetite and severe pain in his left loin. He was admitted to a small cottage hospital and then transferred to the University Hospital in Ljubljana under the care of my friend, Professor Miro Kosak. Investigations showed that he had complete obstruction to the outlet from his left kidney and laparotomy was necessary to determine its cause. I spoke several times on the telephone to Miro Kosak and told him that when he decided to operate I would come over.

The operation was arranged for Friday, November 24th. The previous day, I flew in the morning from Leeds-Bradford airport to Heathrow, then caught the mid-day flight to Zagreb, where a car was waiting for me. In the late afternoon, after we had crossed the Alps, the weather became very bad with snow and fog. Our pilot considered it unsafe to land at Zagreb so decided to take us to Belgrade.

In Belgrade it was already dark and snowing heavily. We were escorted into buses which would take us approximately two hundred miles to Zagreb and Ljubljana. However, the weather worsened, and about ten miles out of Belgrade the buses had to turn back. This time we were taken to the railway station and given tickets for a train which left about midnight.

I sat up all night having a corner seat in a second class compartment, and slept very little. We did not arrive in Ljubljana until 10.00 am the following morning. A car was waiting for me and I was immediately taken to the hospital.

In the operating suite, while I was changing my clothes, Miro Kosak came in and asked me to operate, he would assist. I told him I had had a hazardous journey and was a bit tired but he eventually persuaded me. I had a chance of greeting Sime before he was anaesthetised, and tried to tell him in Italian that everything would be fine.

But alas, his abdominal cavity was covered all over with small secondary carcinoma, the primary appeared to have started in the stomach. Sadly there was nothing we could do.

After I had washed and changed, Sime had recovered consciousness, so I went to speak to him. I shall never forget my last meeting with him, tears were in his eyes when he grasped my hand, kissed it and thanked me. There was little I could say without betraying my grief, but I did reassure him and told him we should be meeting again soon in Korcula. This was not to be, two weeks after the operation he was taken back to Korcula and died there after being at home only three weeks.

After we had finished at the hospital, and changed and dressed, Miro Kosak invited me to his house. He discovered that the airport was likely to be closed for a few days and advised me to travel by train to Munich and fly back from there. We went to the station, bought a ticket and discovered that the train left at about 11.00 pm. I spent the afternoon asleep on a couch in Miro's house. In the evening his wife cooked an excellent meal for us and we drank a lot of wine — probably a bit too much — when I told them it was my birthday. Under normal circumstances we had allowed sufficient time to get to the station, but it was still snowing and there was already six inches of it on the road.

Miro then had difficulty in starting his car which had been left in the open, but eventually it responded and we set off. Fortunately, his son had come with us, because soon we required his help. When we were about five hundred yards from the railway station the car stopped again and refused to start. Miro told his son to carry my suitcase, run to the station and hold up the train until we arrived. We quickly followed — and I thought as I ran that if I survive until I reach the train, I shall never ever have a heart attack.

I was completely drenched when I arrived. I managed to obtain a place in a four-berth compartment with three other men, so did not feel embarrassed when I changed all my clothes in front of them.

Early next morning we arrived at Munich in thick fog. The information desk at the station informed me that the airport was closed, and advised me to take the so-called breakfast train to Frankfurt, which I did, travelling in great comfort and having an excellent breakfast.

In Frankfurt the skies were clear and there was brilliant sunshine. I took a taxi to the airport, obtained a flight on a South African plane to Heathrow and flew back from London to Leeds. I had been away only two days, but it felt like a month.

Sime Dominkovic was a great character and the most popular person in Korcula. Practically everyone attended his funeral, filling the cathedral completely. But the tragic events for his family had not finished: during the funeral service his brother-in-law, who for some time had been treated for indigestion, had a severe heart attack and died in the vestry of the cathedral while the service was taking place.

Before Tito severed links with Stalin, I was in Korcula for a few days, and I was informed that there was a political meeting in the cinema, which everybody must attend, so I accompanied my friends to see what a Communist meeting was really like. The cinema was absolutely full, we managed to find seats but many people were standing.

The orator was a Serb who had come from Belgrade to address this meeting. He had a miserable face, smoked cigarettes the whole time, and continued in a monotonous voice reading most of what he had to say, for over three hours. Nobody left until he had finished.

About five years later after Tito had quarrelled with Stalin there was another political meeting in the cinema — being addressed by the same monotonous speaker whom I had seen previously. Now only about thirty people were listening to him, most of the inhabitants of Korcula were outside on the terrace drinking beer or coffee.

During the Stalin era the local stores were short of many commodities, so I usually travelled by car, enabling me to carry soap, washing powder, tea etc. On one occasion I took fourteen pounds of margarine in the boot of the Austin Westminster. When I arrived in Korcula only a small amount of liquid margarine remained on the floor of the boot, all the remainder had escaped leaving a trail across Europe, from Ostend to Korcula. The two doctors who had travelled with me had noticed an 'oil leak' but thinking it was because the engine was hot, they did not wish to disturb me, and said nothing.

One summer I invited some Scottish friends, Helen and Simon Grieve, to come and stay with me. They had a villa near my house in Italy, and their daughter Fiona worked at our Embassy in Rome. When they arrived in Korcula, Simon looked ill and the following day his condition worsened rapidly. He was admitted to Dubrovnik Hospital and two days later, he unfortunately died of acute pancreatitis. I joined Helen in Dubrovnik to help all that I could. She was a member of the Church of Scotland, and would not even tolerate the Protestant religion, but nothing could be worse than being a Roman Catholic. From the hotel in Dubrovnik we telephoned our Consul in Split and then our Embassy in Belgrade. We were informed that a Protestant priest was attached to our Embassy, but he was on holiday in England, and a Catholic priest was acting for him. Helen looked furious and answered nothing. Then we went to the cemetery to speak to the sexton and to arrange the service and burial. He asked Helen whether she wanted her husband buried in the Christian or in the Moslem part of the cemetery, which could not have been less tactful and completely floored her, I thought she would faint. She turned to me saying: 'You must take the service'. I wasn't sure whether this was allowed but enquired at the Mayor's office in Dubrovnik and after a lengthy delay they agreed, saying that they had never had such a request before.

Returning to my hotel, I was wondering whether I had made a mistake. I had no prayer book, no Bible, in fact nothing religious except what I could remember of the Lord's Prayer. After dinner I wrote down a few notes and corrected what I had written several times before I thought it would be ecclesiastically acceptable. Next morning I escorted Helen to the small church in the cemetery and soon the pall bearers arrived carrying a black plastic coffin. Helen looked very annoyed, saying to me: 'It's second hand'. I conducted the service as well as I could, I am sure it was the shortest burial service on record. Then we went out to the burial ground. Two grave diggers were working extremely hard trying to make the site deep enough through what appeared to be solid rock, when one of them lost his trousers. He had nothing to secure them with until I gave him a piece of string.

The next day Helen flew back to London, and I returned to Korcula to rest for a few days in my house, which I badly needed.

There is an interesting story about two brothers who lived in Korcula during the 16th Century. They were orphans called Vinko and Anton Paletin: Vinko the elder boy was adventurous and in 1530 boarded a Spanish ship hoping to reach Mexico. The ship was wrecked on the peninsula of Yukatan and Vinko swam ashore. He arrived penniless — so joined the Spanish army for four years. After his army career he became a Dominican monk, and returned to Europe in about 1540. His final years were spent at the Dominican monastery of St. Nicola in Korcula.

Anton, the younger brother, was captured by the Turks while travelling by ship to Dubrovnik. He was taken to Istanbul, and converted to Islam. He became one of the most successful of the Turkish naval commanders, and changed his name to Jusut. In 1571, the Turkish government decided to take Korcula. On August 15th, Jusut arrived with the Turkish fleet off the Dalmation coast near to the city. He secretly contacted his brother Vinko telling him their plan of attack, resulting in the Turkish fleet having to retire.

Lord and Lady Bolton join the welcoming party for the Yugoslav Olympic swimming team at West Burton.

Moreska Dancers from Korcula helped the British Heart Foundation (Wensleydale Group) in 1980 by giving a performance at Bolton Hall, and the following day performed in Leeds Civic Hall.

Some believe that the Korculeans swam out during one night and made holes in the Turkish ships which sank, and the reason why Anton came to Korcula was to convert his brother to Islam, so saving him from eternal damnation.

I have noticed that the Korculeans do display an extraordinary power of buoyancy, and are very strong swimmers. You see them walk into the sea or dive in and then appear to sit on the water, chatting to one another, as one does in one's sitting room. Half their body is always above the water.

My nephew, Andrew Hepper, discovered that the only way of ducking them after they had been aggressive to him was to dive and pull them down with their feet. It was a technique which gained him many good friends.

In the summer of 1969 the Yugoslav Olympic swimming team was competing against the British at the new International Swimming Pool in Leeds. The whole team came to stay a night with me at West Burton, and Lord and Lady Bolton helped me entertain them.

BRITISH HEART FOUNDATION
Wensleydale Group
90 MORESKA DANCERS
(Yugoslavian)
3 GROUPS—ORCHESTRA—FOLK SINGERS
at BOLTON HALL
by kind permission of Lord Bolton
at 1 o'clock
NATIONAL SPIT ROAST — WINE BAR, BEER, SOFT DRINKS
on
SUNDAY, OCTOBER 5th, 1980
Tickets £2·00
Application for Tickets must be made before September 29th, 1980
to MRS. D. A. HUNT,
Burton House,
Masham, Nr. Ripon, North Yorkshire
HG4 4BP
Please enclose a stamped addressed envelope.

SUNDAY, OCTOBER 5th, 1980
Please send me.................................Tickets
I enclose a cheque for.................................
or donation
Name ....
Address ....
....

The Korculeans have a folk dancing team, which is internationally famous, and is called the Moreska Dancers. They have visited Yorkshire on two occasions, the last being in 1980 when they gave a performance at Bolton Hall in aid of the British Heart Foundation.

Korcula is an extremely attractive town, it is really like a miniature Venice, but without canals. I prefer it to Dubrovnik because, being situated on an island, and a long way from an airport, it never has too many visitors. There is always something to attract your attention and provide enjoyment. The people are gifted in so many ways.

On saint days there is a religious procession through the old city. The procession on an Easter Sunday is reported to be the longest in Europe, attracting many visitors, which has earned Korcula the title of 'Little Rome'.

My house is in the centre of the old town near to the Cathedral, and so it is close to where most of the activities take place.

You never have a dull moment in Korcula, and I continue to have many happy times there.

17

How Not To Run a Restaurant

Surgeons from many different countries had been to see our work at the Leeds Infirmary and on occasions I would take them to my country house in Wensleydale for the weekend. I was surprised to discover how many of them were interested in cooking. At first I knew little about it myself because I was never allowed into the kitchen when I was young, but the variety of dishes which were served at the weekends in Wensleydale began to interest me and I took a particular liking to Hungarian cuisine.

I had for some years owned a property in Headingley which consisted of twenty flats with a restaurant on the ground floor. I thought it would be interesting to refurbish the whole building, make the restaurant attractive, and to run it myself. Two of my friends who heard about this new venture came to see me. The first was Lord Hacking, a Director of the hotel chain Trust Houses, and he strongly advised me against it, as did Bernard Cayzer, who had just built three hotels in the Canary Isles. But I like a challenge and would not have embarked on heart surgery had I been easily frightened. So, the Headingley building was renovated, with new bathrooms for every flat and a new kitchen built, etc.

I appointed a young chef who had been trained at the Cardinal Restaurant in Wetherby. His father was a policeman and he himself stood at least six feet four inches in height. Not knowing the requirements for a restaurant, I gave the chef a free hand to buy everything for the kitchen and the adjoining storerooms. He naturally had all the cupboards and equipment fitted to suit his size so that he would not need to bend. However, just before we were about to open, he left, having decided to join his father in the police force. The next chef who answered our advertisement was no more than five foot six inches tall, and quite unable to reach anything. He stayed just long enough for all the fittings in the kitchen to be adjusted to his size and then he left.

I began to discover that chefs are very temperamental people and easily upset, particularly when they are asked to use a cooker which they didn't order themselves. As the chefs changed frequently, I acquired a collection of cookers which I kept in the stables at the back of the restaurant, so when a new chef arrived I took him there to inspect the collection and asked him which one he preferred.

Mrs. Conyers, a friend of mine, realising I was having a bit of trouble, came to help me run the restaurant. We both had had considerable experience of entertaining our friends at home but really no idea how to run a profitable business. We could not understand why the local restauranteurs came each evening repeatedly asking for Napoleon brandies and it was only after a few weeks we discovered that we were selling it at a lower price than we could buy it ourselves.

My surgical team at the Leeds Infirmary had known for a long time that I was no good at mathematics so when I left them they gave me an adding machine as a farewell present. The first time I used it was when some of the Leeds United football team came into the bar and I chose to serve them. They ordered three beers and a whisky. I proudly produced my new machine, tapped out the prices and obtained a surprising result of £365.00, which prompted me to remark 'Good gracious, I can afford a car'. I had tapped out the multiplication tag instead of the addition one.

I think we had five chefs during the one year we were open. The first one, who decided to become a policeman, was honest, but that could not be said for all the others, some of whom had considerable experience in other pursuits as well as cooking. One was a good chef, he had trained in France, but he was crafty. We agreed to allow him a small percentage on all meat and fish he ordered for the restaurant. One Sunday morning when there was no staff about, I inspected the waste bins and found a whole suckling pig and more than half a turkey thrown away. I took them with me to the Dales, washed them, and then made some delicious meatballs which I brought back to Leeds, asking the chef to sample my cooking. He apologised profoundly when I told him the recipe, and I thought that all would be well after this episode but, a little later on, the police informed me that they had proof the chef was selling our meat to the night clubs in Huddersfield and they wanted me to prosecute him. My brother, who was my solicitor, and who had just relinquished his post as Lord Mayor of Leeds, refused to allow me to do so. He said we had had enough publicity and did not seek any more.

Apart from the chefs, the restaurant was fraught with misfortune from the beginning, for it was partly responsible for my being disqualified from driving for a year. Just before we opened, a Leeds wine merchant brought a considerable quantity of wine for us to sample and so decide which to order. We had sampled about seven different bottles when I thought I had had about enough. There still remained at least five which we had not tried. Driving back to my house in Clarendon Road I clipped the corner as I turned into Reservoir Street. A police car stopped me and the tests showed that I was above the limit. I was issued with a summons, which I immediately took to my brother. The next morning, the young policeman who had arrested me came to the restaurant with a fellow policeman. They apologised for what they had done and asked me to return the summons to them so that they could destroy it. I telephoned my brother at his office, but he refused to release it, saying that I must face the consequences.

I showed both of them into the bar where the wine tasting had taken place, offering them to sample one of the bottles that had not been opened. Only the young policeman tasted. I noticed that he immediately changed colour and declined to finish it. When they had both left I thought I would taste the wine myself and discovered that I had served neat whisky. The bar was in a dark part of the restaurant where it was difficult to see anything without using electric light.

Three months later, I attended the Magistrates' Court in Leeds Town Hall. The young policeman surprisingly turned up and escorted me into the Court room, apologising all the way. The Stipendiary Magistrate took my case and asked me a few questions, then obviously knowing something about wine himself, he said, 'Surely, Mr. Wooler when you are tasting wine you spit it out and do not swallow it'. My reply was 'What a dreadful waste' and this caused so much amusement in the Court that no more questions were asked. I was fined £30.00 and was disqualified from driving for a year.

I needed a car and so I employed as driver a young man who had been working at Bolton Castle. Before the Spring I received a message from Southern Italy to say my villa had been broken into and some of the contents had been stolen. The Italian police asked me to go over and detail what was missing so I went by road, my newly engaged driver taking me the fifteen hundred miles to Southern Italy and the fifteen hundred miles back.

On returning to Yorkshire my driver, after celebrating his first journey by car to Italy with some of his friends, was stopped on his way home, breathalysed and found to be over the limit, but the police discovered as well that he had no driving licence. It had expired six months previously and he had forgotten to renew it, so I had been driven from North Yorkshire to Calabria and back by someone without a licence.

It soon became obvious that I was not enjoying my new occupation of trying to be a restauranteur, nor was I being successful. Previously, entertaining my surgical friends at home, I had been accustomed to having just one party every week, usually on a Saturday evening, but now with the restaurant opened every day we were having two parties a day, presumably in order to keep our customers amused. If I hid myself away in my private room to read and be quiet, invariably one of the staff would come to me saying 'You must come and see so and so and speak to him in the bar. He is very important and has asked for you'.

Entertaining my friends in the Dales was enjoyable but entertaining as a business in order to make a profit was a different matter. I found it difficult to be polite to some of my customers. I well remember a middle-aged couple coming into the bar when the barman, who was Peter Milostic, had retired for a smoke; I had taken over from him and prepared to serve our two guests. The husband had an expressionless face which only moved when he drank his whisky. His wife was wearing far too much jewellery. If it was real it was ridiculous, and if it was artificial it was very vulgar. The wife, speaking in a loud voice, so that everybody in the bar could hear her, described how they had spent a few thousand pounds on a trip to America, taking the State rooms on the Queen Mary and staying at the Ritz Hotel in New York, etc. I turned away not wishing to hear such nonsense. Then when she saw that I was not paying attention, she rapped the bar counter, ordering some ridiculous American cocktail. I told her that I had not a clue what she required. One of the waiters saw that I was being difficult, and, understanding her language, came in and served her with the absurd cocktail. He then returned to the restaurant. There was a pause, then another rap on the bar counter, she asked for a match to light a gold-tip black cigarette. I had taken an intense dislike to her and really could not tolerate her so I told her that I had no matches and that I didn't encourage smoking because I had removed far too many lungs. Mrs. Conyers came in to defuse the situation and I returned to my room for peace but, later on in the same evening, I spoke to Mrs. Conyers and told her that I had just about had enough of this restaurant business. It was something I wasn't used to and I was really hating every moment.

I had tried to run the restaurant for only one year but during that time it had accumulated a vast overdraft which no doubt pleased the directors of Barclays Bank because they knew that my other assets could more than meet the consequences.

So after a disastrous year running the restaurant, I more or less gave the business to the head chef, allowing him to continue in the building as a tenant. I left Leeds and went to live at my country house in the Yorkshire Dales.

18

Peace at Last

The Grange at West Burton is in a strategic position where three valleys meet — Wensleydale, Bishopdale and the Walden valley. I was told that it was originally a farm belonging to Coverham Abbey. Before a packhorse bridge was built, the road from West Burton crossed the Walden Beck by a ford which still exists directly in front of the house, then it continues up the side of Pen Hill to Coverham Abbey.

A painting of the house in 1710 shows that it had been built in an attractive mansion style, when it belonged to a Huguenot family — the Costabadie. A banking family called Wynn bought it in 1867 and Victorianised it as we see it today.

The gardens are most attractive. The rock garden was designed by Hilliers who also built the one at Sandringham House. The different colours and shapes of the plants and trees fascinated me. I became particularly interested in alpines and shrubs. I made many friends amongst the gardening community who followed the advice of the late Mr George Knight, chairman of the Northern Horticultural Society. He used to say: 'Good plants should be given away, and bad plants thrown away'.

The gardens at St Nicholas near Richmond are packed with rare plants and shrubs collected by the late Hon. Robert James — who, when alive, was considered to be the best amateur gardener in the country. His widow, the Lady Serena James, became one of my great friends and I made good use of her husband's collection. I never visited St Nicholas without a pair of secateurs and a plastic bag, Lady Serena always encouraging me to help myself, the result being that the gardens at West Burton and also the gardens here in Leeds are full of St Nicholas achievements.

My gardening exploits ended in 1993 when I had my first heart attack. I had been collecting used sewing machines to send to my friends in Croatia who were fighting the Serbs. After collecting 27 machines, my heart had had enough, and went into failure. I was admitted to the Leeds General Infirmary and after a cardioversion I had a pacemaker implanted. This was renewed earlier this year, 1998.

Members of the Wooler Society on tour through Austria, Hungary, Roumania and Yugoslavia.

GEOFFREY H. WOOLER

CONSULTANT SURGEON TO THE THORACIC SURGICAL DEPT

GENERAL INFIRMARY AT LEEDS

(1948-1976)

PRESENTED BY MEMBERS OF THE WOOLER SOCIETY

AUGUST 8th 1989

A plaque at the entrance to Leeds General Infirmary provided by the Wooler Society.

Lady Serena James showing HRH Princess Alice, Duchess of Gloucester, her garden at St Nicholas, Richmond, North Yorkshire.

Although I am unable to work in the garden myself, I have two young fit men who are prepared to listen to my advice and fortunately believe what I say — we have no problems. So I just walk around the garden each morning looking at the plants in the same way as I had been used to doing a ward round at the hospital — accompanied by my two assistants who could legitimately be called gardening houseman and gardening registrar.

I have been very lucky with almost all my friendships in the medical profession. The surgeons who worked with me at the Leeds General Infirmary enjoyed their time so much, they did not wish to lost contact when their appointment had finished. Unknown to me they formed a group which they named 'The Wooler Society'. It meets every year to renew old memories, and is always a most enjoyable success.

In 1989, to commemorate the annual meetings, the American members brought a plaque which, to my surprise, was fixed on a wall at the main entrance to the General Infirmary at Leeds.

In the Society as in all aspects of life I have been fortunate to have so many good friends.

Postscript

Variety is the Spice of Life

Two of my friends, who have kindly read and corrected the page proofs of this book, bitterly complain that I have written very little about my own work since arriving in Leeds, so I have added the following account, and because it is of a clinical nature, I have had to use some surgical terminology.

I was the last honorary surgeon to be appointed to the staff of the Leeds General Infirmary before the Health Service commenced. Mr Philip Allison was the surgeon in charge of the thoracic surgical department, and his influence covered a large area of Yorkshire, which included Bradford, Halifax, Huddersfield, Hull, York and sanatoria as far afield as Aysgarth in North Yorkshire.

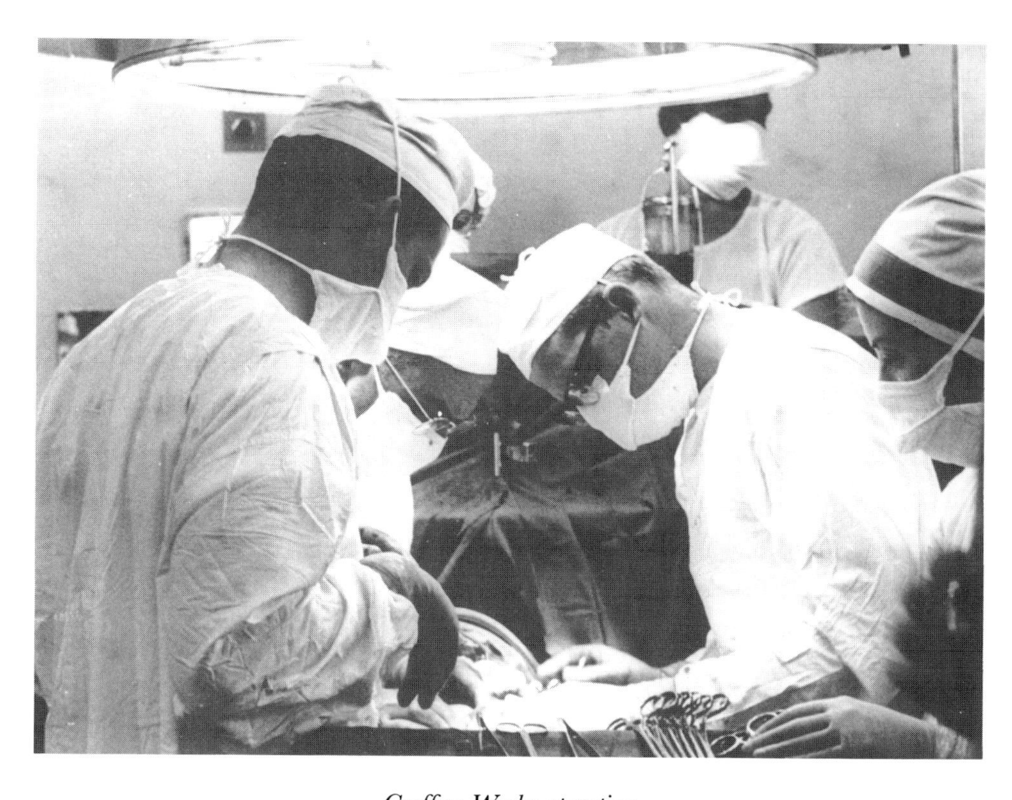

Geoffrey Wooler operating.

There were thoracic surgical teams working at Killingbeck Hospital, Leeds, Pinderfields Hospital, near Wakefield, and Scotton Banks Hospital, near Knaresborough, all controlled by the surgeons at the L.G.I., Mr Allison, Mr John Aylwin and myself. Coverage of such a large area brought a great number of different disorders to be treated.

The policy was to improve the treatment of one particular condition at a time, along with routine work. This was Mr Allison's method, and the variety of cases prevented us from becoming bored. When I arrived in Leeds, Philip Allison was concentrating on cancer of the stomach and oesophagus (food-pipe). He advocated removing most of the organs surrounding the stomach which might have cancer cells in them. It was a lengthy procedure. The only satisfaction to the surgeon was that after a very long operation he finished with a very large specimen, making it easy to close the wound. I assisted with two of these operations, and then he asked me to do one myself. My previous gastric experience was limited. I had removed only small portions of the stomach; but this time, the whole stomach and most of the surrounding structures had to go as well. It took me over six hours, but I succeeded, and was rewarded with a bottle of beer from Philip. The patient and myself both survived.

I should like to mention some of the disorders we were dealing with at that time. We had a large number of cases of hiatal hernia, more than were published at the Mayo Clinic in Rochester, USA. Our friends in London used to joke about this apparently common condition in Yorkshire, and they named it the Leeds Disease.

At least one resection of the oesophagus for peptic stricture or cancer was performed every week. We always used small intestine for replacement, and I never saw a post-operative leak, even though on two occasions the small intestine was brought up as high as the neck.

We did not rely on other people's diagnoses, and always investigated the patients ourselves, so that every week at least 12 oesophagoscopies and even more bronchoscopies were performed to clinch the diagnosis before recommending surgery. Cardiac catheterisation was first performed at the L.G.I. by the surgeons in the thoracic surgical department. It took several weeks to persuade the cardiologists that they could safely handle this for themselves.

Lung resections for carcinoma or tubercle were a daily occurrence, and again I never remember seeing a post-operative bronchial leak. A straightforward pneumoectomy for cancer used to take me less than an hour.

One of my first private patients was Mr T.L. Taylor, President of the Yorkshire County Cricket Club. He had a narrowing of his oesophagus, the opening being no more than about a quarter of an inch in diameter, but he was not

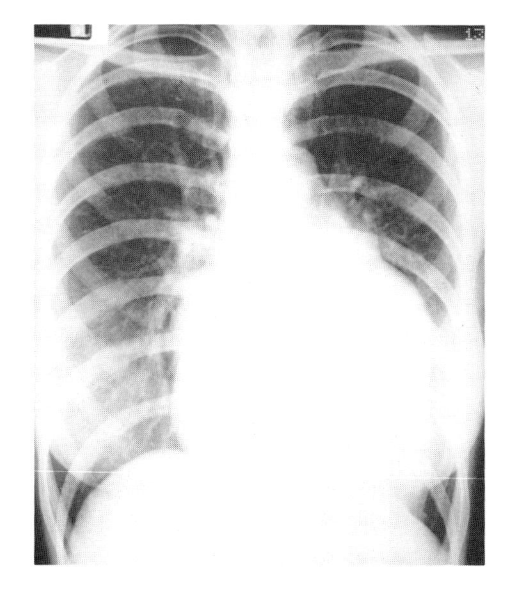

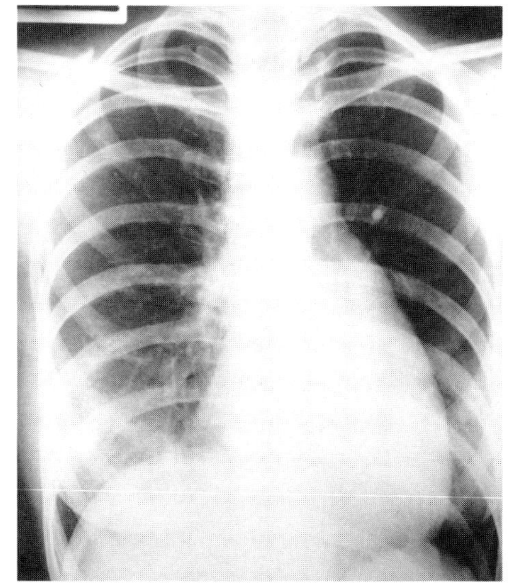

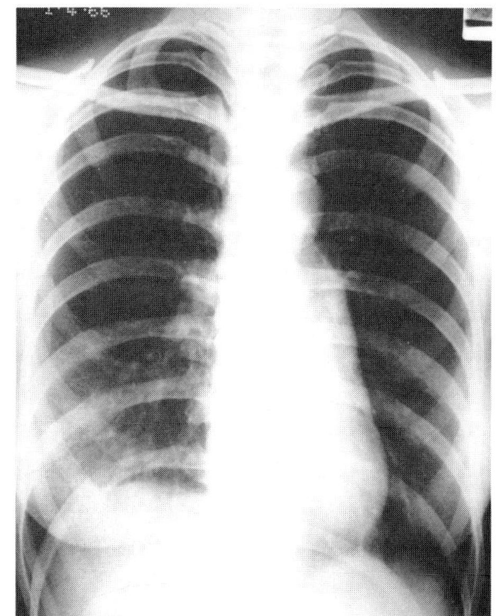

Three photographs illustrate the success achieved by repairing a mitral heart valve. The first (top left) is pre-operation and shows great enlargement of the heart. The second (above) was taken three months later after the operation, and the heart has diminished in size. The third (left), taken a year after surgery, shows a heart looking normal.

wasted; if anything, he was a bit over-weight. I asked him how he managed to remain so well nourished, and he gave me this answer: his cook steamed a chicken in a pressure cooker, then she put it through the mincer, bones and all, and mashed the result while adding condiments and some cream. His butler finished the recipe by pouring half a bottle of port over the mashed chicken. Mr Taylor proudly announced to me that he drank a whole chicken every day.

In 1954, I spoke at the annual meeting of the French Surgical Society in Paris about obstructions to the oesophagus. After the meeting, the farewell banquet was held at a restaurant in the Champs Elysees. We were in the foyer talking when we noticed that a friend's trouser zip had wandered and he was showing the front tail of his shirt. It was at a time when zips were in their infancy, and not very secure. We shielded him while he adjusted himself, and then went into the banqueting hall. He sat opposite me at the dinner table, and when the speeches had ended I reminded him to check his zip. He found it had wandered again, and so adjusted it, but when he left the table he took the table cloth with him! Before leaving the restaurant I introduced myself to the head chef. He conducted me into the kitchens, and showed me the correct way to make French onion soup which I have found most useful when entertaining my friends in Yorkshire.

Children with congenital oesophageal atresia (malformation) were always referred to us for treatment, and I enjoyed reconstructing their oesophagi. Many cases of oesophageal varices caused by liver cirrhosis were referred to our unit. Mr Allison devised a method of devascularising the oesophagus, whereas I favoured performing a porta-caval side-to-side anastomosis. Professor Sheila Sherlock sent us cases from London which required surgery.

In 1952, I managed to excise successfully a large aneurysm (rupture) of the left ventricle of the heart before a heart-lung machine was available. In 1954, two years before you could buy a heart-lung machine, I had a patient with a syphilitic aneurysm of the ascending aorta — which is very close to the heart. It had continued to grow steadily and had eroded through the sternum (breast-bone), and presented as a large pulsating tumour on the front of his chest. One day I saw this patient while shopping in Leeds, and noticed that his necktie was pushed forward and pulsating with each heart beat. I advised him not to cough.

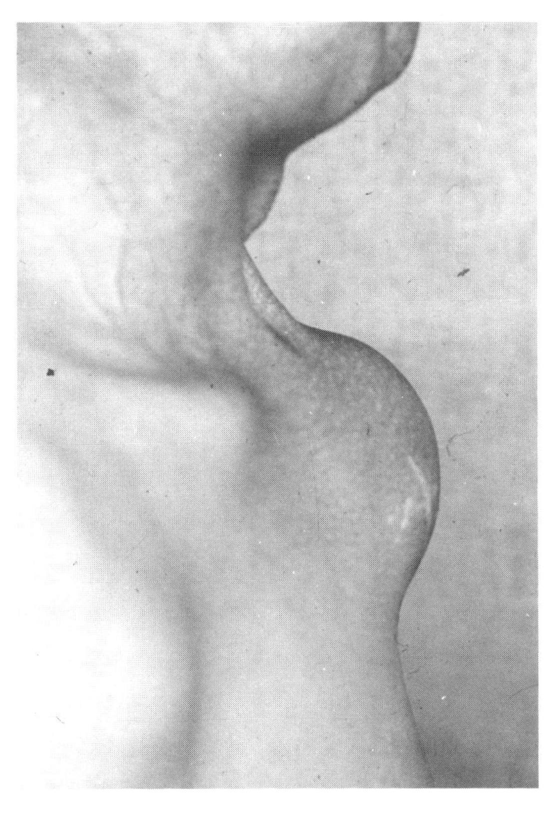

The photograph shows an aneurysm ruptured through the breast-bone.

Shortly afterwards, I was asked to operate on him because he was becoming so short of breath.

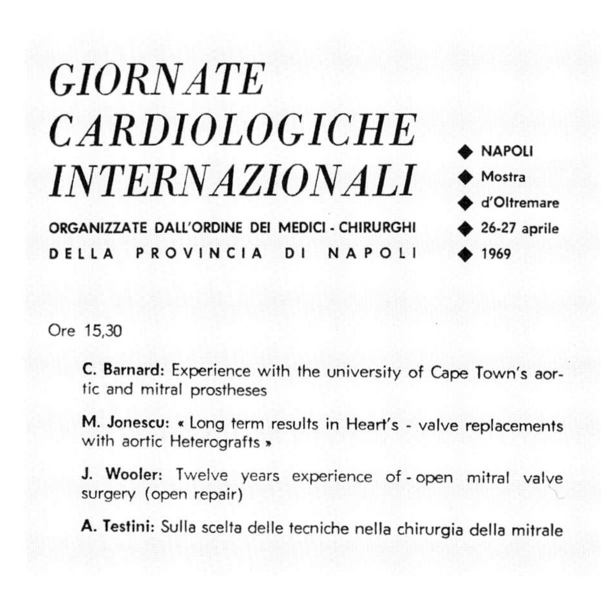

GIORNATE CARDIOLOGICHE INTERNAZIONALI

ORGANIZZATE DALL'ORDINE DEI MEDICI - CHIRURGHI DELLA PROVINCIA DI NAPOLI

◆ NAPOLI ◆ Mostra ◆ d'Oltremare ◆ 26-27 aprile ◆ 1969

Ore 15,30

C. Barnard: Experience with the university of Cape Town's aortic and mitral prostheses

M. Jonescu: « Long term results in Heart's - valve replacements with aortic Heterografts »

J. Wooler: Twelve years experience of - open mitral valve surgery (open repair)

A. Testini: Sulla scelta delle tecniche nella chirurgia della mitrale

Twelve years of experience in 1969 ... and they nearly got the name right.

Freeing the aneurysm from surrounding structures took six hours, and because it had lost all support, it expanded rapidly in size, blowing up with blood like a balloon. Unfortunately, I stabbed my left index finger with the scalpel while dissecting. After applying a dressing inside my rubber glove, I carried on.

When the aneurysm was completely free, we thought we had won, and that the worst part of the operation was over. All that remained was to apply clamps across the neck of the aneurysm, excise it, and stitch up the hole. Unfortunately, when the clamps were applied, we squeezed blood clots into the circulation, from which the patient did not recover. This could have been avoided had we had a heart-lung machine, and used it with Charles Drew's method of deep cooling. It would have enabled us to divert the blood flow from the heart, and indeed stop the circulation completely for a short time. Because I had stabbed my finger and drawn blood while operating on a syphilitic patient, my blood had to be tested frequently for a whole year. Fortunately, I was eventually discharged, having escaped a dreaded infection. During the whole of my career, this was the only time when I cut myself while operating, and I had chosen a syphilitic patient.

We commenced closed-heart surgery in 1948, doing mitral valvotomies, coarctation of the aorta, closing a patent ductus, and 'de-coking' the heart for constrictive pericarditis. The next stage was to cool the patient in a bath of iced water, and then apply tourniquets around the venea cavae to produce an inflow occlusion and stop the blood flow; you then had about ten minutes to deal with simple lesions inside the heart. As I have already recounted, we bought a Melrose heart-lung machine in 1956. All accessories such as catheters, tubing, etc had to be made or begged from the Americans because they were unobtainable in Britain. In February, 1957, we had a success repairing a mitral heart valve, which was leaking. It was the second case in the world that had been successful. We quickly acquired a reputation for repairing heart valves,

Geoffrey Wooler at a conference in Italy, 1969.

The first meeting of the Wooler Society at the Grange, West Burton, in August, 1983.

A friend, Juna Valentokevic, w'
'small' catch for Korcula.

A photograph taken two years ago in Korcula. With Geoffrey Wooler is a friend, Anna-Maria Vanacore.

and cases arrived from almost every country. Many valves were so badly damaged that they could not be repaired and had to be replaced. An American, Albert Starr, produced a ball valve prosthesis, which has proved invaluable, and is still in use today.

Marian Ionescu joined my unit in Leeds and worked on heterographs (animal tissue replacements) to replace baldy damaged heart valves. He had great success using calf pericardium to make valve leaflets which he mounted on a metal frame.

At about this time I decided to retire.

Tuberculosis had been eradicated. Patients with lung cancer were diminishing in number. Cancer of the stomach and oesophagus was being dealt with by general surgeons. Coronary artery surgery was just coming into fashion — with a flood of cases; there was little time to do anything else. The daily repetition of similar operations did not interest me, and so I retired to the Yorkshire Dales.

It has been comforting to know that at least some of my patients are alive 23 years afterwards, because they telephone me, expressing surprise that I am still alive too.

December 1998